MARIE DE ROHAN

1. The Duchesse de Chevreuse (Marie de Rohan), from a portrait by Moreelsi, once in the possession of Charles I

MARIE DE ROHAN
Duchesse de Chevreuse

by Michael Prawdin

London · George Allen & Unwin Ltd
RUSKIN HOUSE · MUSEUM STREET

© George Allen & Unwin Ltd 1971

ISBN 0 04 923053 0

Printed in Great Britain
in 11 point Plantin
by Cox & Wyman Ltd, Fakenham

Preface

Marie de Rohan – as Mme de Chevreuse – was for more than thirty years one of the most important factors in French politics. Those three decades were the crucial transitional period in which Richelieu, and after him Mazarin, were at work to create the conditions for the establishment of the absolute monarchy in France, which meant breaking the power of the semi-independent feudal lords in the different provinces. They both tried to win Marie to their cause but she, herself belonging to the highest aristocracy, detested their dictatorial presumptions, and when they recognized that she could not be won over they treated her as a formidable and dangerous enemy.

At first her motive was not political: it was her concern for the well-being and safety of her friend, the young Queen Anne, who, unloved and distrusted by her husband, Louis XIII, lived in constant anxiety about her future. To discover Richelieu's intentions regarding the Queen, there could be only one way: to win over one of his closest and most trusted collaborators, which meant inducing him to risk his own security and high position for no tangible advantage whatsoever. But Marie, sure of her irresistible charm, set to work and succeeded. As one of her contemporaries wrote: 'Nothing is impossible for a woman who is so beautiful and so spirited as this one.'

When their clandestine connection was discovered, through her collaborator's lack of caution, she was banished from Court; but from her enforced residence in a remote province she constantly increased her political activity against Richelieu's dictatorship. When, later on, new investigations into the attitudes of the Queen and her adherents began, Marie risked her life by riding through France in disguise to seek refuge in England, where she was welcomed by the Court of Charles I and from where she continued with her fight against Richelieu's regime.

Even more than by Richelieu, who could not fail to be impressed by her abilities, she was hated by Louis XIII, and after Richelieu's

7

death the King's hatred increased. In his last will he excluded her from any pardon and when the document was read to him before being put to Parlement to become law, the dying monarch raised his emaciated hand and exclaimed in a croaking voice: 'This woman is the devil! She is the devil! The very devil!'

Now Mazarin took over the Government for the Queen-Regent, and when circumstances forced him to recall Marie to France he offered her the greatest advantages in order to win her to his policy. But she demanded the reinstatement of the great nobles in their old positions with their ancient privileges, and soon she had once more to flee from the country.

When the Fronde, the mainly Parisian insurrection against the dictatorial regime of Mazarin, gained strength, she returned and became the brain and soul of the movement. But very soon she proved that her fight was not primarily directed against the Government but against anyone who aspired to a position of dictatorship; against such a threat she was even prepared to ally herself with the Government, using her influence to make it more conciliatory.

However, in the end she had to recognize that the whole character of the aristocracy itself had changed. The nobles, whether of the Fronde or not, showed no interest in their class, but sought only their individual personal advantages; so she gave up the struggle. Yet her relentless fight, her complete disdain for danger and risk, though she was not backed by any powerful party, acting on her own according to her personal judgement of the situation, did not fail to arouse general interest. Mazarin himself wrote of her, 'She has a clear conception of everything and is never discouraged,' and the greatest adventurer of the time, later Cardinal de Retz, acknowledged that 'she often suggested such brilliant expedients that they seemed like flashes of lightning'.

Her courage and the strength and fascination of her personality made an unforgettable impression on her contemporaries, and for a generation all memoirs, diaries, notebooks were full either of her condemnation or praise. Only when nationalism and absolutism became established did the historians of the new regime lose interest in preserving the memory of this resolute opponent of their system. It was in the nineteenth century, when liberalistic trends gained influence, that a historian ventured to show her as

8

an idealistic fighter for the rights of her class against oppression; but later historical writers, up to the present time, have not concerned themselves with her motives and intentions. It was the fascinating woman of irresistible charm, and her amorous adventures, that stirred their imagination and they described her simply as an intriguer with no other purpose than the mere enjoyment of intrigues.

This book tries to give a balanced picture of the personality of Marie de Rohan, one of the great political women that France has produced, and to show the historical circumstances which drove her to action.

Contents

Illustrations

Nos. 1, 2, 7, 8, 9, 10, 11, were supplied by the Mansell Collection

Chapter I

When on April 24, 1617, the news spread that Concini had been killed, all Paris went wild with joy, for this Italian upstart was universally hated. He had come to France during the reign of Henri IV, had secured for himself the position of Master of the Horse to the Queen, Marie de Medici, and had then worked his way into her favour. When after the assassination of the King she became Queen Regent for her nine-year-old son, she bestowed on Concini the title of marquis, then that of Marshal of France; eventually he became to all intents and purposes the country's ruler. With every promotion his rapacity and arrogance had grown more intolerable.

The nobles therefore forced the Queen to convoke the Estates General, but their division into three classes – nobles, clergy and third estate – each with its own grievances and demands, filled the meetings with futile quarrels. Finally the assembly was easily dissolved without achieving anything, leaving Concini's government in power to rule as before. During the convocation the thirteen-year-old King, Louis XIII, was declared of age, and at the public declaration of his majority he confirmed in Parlement his mother's power 'to govern and command as hitherto' just as she had ordered him to do.

The boy-king lived in continual dread of his mother and her fits of temper, which were accompanied by severe punishment. He stammered and was regarded as intellectually backward. So she encouraged him to spend his days hunting and hawking, pastimes of which he was very fond. When the weather was bad, he made his dogs draw his toy cannons through the corridors of the Louvre and he fired them from the balconies. Among the attendants chosen for him was a man of the petty provincial nobility, Charles Albert de Luynes, who was in his late thirties but looked younger. He had won the affections of the boy-king. He was an expert falconer, took an eager part in the amusements of his little master and, fully understanding the suppressed bitterness of the boy's feelings, aroused in him a deep resentment and anger against the treatment accorded to him by his mother and Concini, who was becoming increasingly insolent and treated with disdain the boy-king, who was kept apart from all matters of state.

As soon as the Estates General were dissolved, the Court departed south for the celebration of the double marriage which the Queen-Regent, in pursuit of the keenly sought Spanish alliance, had arranged: that of Louis to the daughter of the King of Spain, Anne of Austria, both of the same age, and at the same time that of his sister, Princess Elisabeth, to Don Felipe (Philip), heir to the Spanish throne.

In spite of all efforts to suppress the gossip, rumours were soon widespread that Louis, now fourteen years old, had, after the marriage festivities, retired to his room and there gone to sleep until he was fetched by his mother and led by her into the nuptial bed, and that the marriage had not been consummated.

Back in Paris, Louis continued the kind of life he had led before, paying only formal, brief visits to his mother and his wife, and it was a very long time before the young pair even had a meal together. But the King remained inseparable from Luynes, and the Queen-Mother could not fail to notice her son's growing sullen opposition and ill-temper. She tried to improve the situation by giving some benefits and promotion to Luynes, but her thoughts were mainly occupied with the rising discontent of various noble factions against her protégé Concini.

So Luynes continued with his tactics and finally convinced Louis that he could not expect the dignity due to his position as sovereign so long as Concini was alive. In the end he obtained the King's agreement to a conspiracy against the dominant Italian. A captain of the Guard, Baron de Vitry, was won to their cause, and when on April 24th Concini, accompanied as usual by a crowd of courtiers, entered the courtyard of the Louvre, Vitry pushed his way through to him and, laying his hand on the favourite's shoulder, declared that he had orders from the King to arrest him. When Concini angrily put his hand to his sword Vitry gave a sign to his men, and they shot the Italian dead. In the momentary excitement and confusion the sixteen-year-old Louis was raised to the window in the gallery with the cry 'Long live the King!' and the nobles, courtiers and soldiers cheered him wildly.

16

2. Marie de Medici, from a portrait by Porbus the younger

3. Louis XIII in early years, from a portrait by Porbus the younger

Now it was Luynes who took control of the country in the King's name. He was created a duke and peer of France; he appropriated all the riches and possessions which Concini had accumulated and filled all the important offices, previously held by Concini's men, with his own adherents. The Queen-Mother, who had been completely dumbfounded by the event, received a message that the King himself would now rule; armed guards appeared at her doors, and she was later ordered to take up residence at the Château de Blois, where her every step was carefully watched. The nobles, who at first had welcomed Concini's assassination and Luynes' assumption of power, hurried to the Court in the expectation that they would be reinstated in their traditional feudal positions; but they were soon disappointed and they returned to their castles, estates and provinces. As one of them remarked: 'Only the sign has been changed; the tavern is still the same.'

At the height of his power, where he now stood, Luynes decided that to enhance his dignity he should form ties with the nobility by marrying, and his choice of bride fell upon Marie de Rohan.

When, nearly two years earlier, the Court of the young Queen Anne was being formed, Marie, the Queen's senior by only ten months, had been appointed a maid-of-honour. Anne, who had been brought up in the strict formality of Spanish etiquette, was at first shocked by the quick wit and sharp tongue of her maid-of-honour who, always ready for pranks and full of fun and surprises, soon became the admired leader of the other French girls in the household. It was not long before Anne, too, began to find pleasure in Marie's lively ways.

The special circumstances of Marie's childhood had encouraged the unrestrained development of her natural inclinations. Her mother died when she was two years old, and her father, Hercule de Rohan, Duc de Montbazon, was always somewhere in the King's service and left her and her brother of four years in the charge of governesses at the Château de Couzières, under the supervision of one of the Duke's mistresses, who is said to have once been a *fille de joie* in the near-by town of Tours. The children grew up wild and unfettered, and defied every attempt at discipline. The two were inseparable and kept the countryside agog with their escapades. Hunting, swimming, fencing, steeplechasing – they risked their necks a dozen times a day with unquenchable zest, and always found preposterously witty answers to all reproaches. Marie often wore her brother's clothes, mixed with his companions and shared his pastimes.

Nevertheless, when at the age of fifteen she came to Anne's Court, she was an enchanting beauty with golden hair, a rather small and dainty figure, slender limbs, and delicate but strong hands. The straight little nose, with quivering, sensitive nostrils, in her oval face, and arched eyebrows and full red lips revealed her temperament. But most alluring were her large, fascinating dark-blue eyes, with absurdly long lashes. They could be dreamy or alight with laughter; at one moment they had a mysterious penetrating power and at the next they were melting and languorous, captivating and haunting. Her loveliness was enhanced by the gaiety, vivacity and spirit, which 'not only shone in her eyes but animated her voice and her gestures, even to her least movements, and imparted to her whole personality an irresistible charm'.

But it was mainly her cheerfulness, her ability to enliven the most gloomy surroundings with some unexpected frolic, which finally won Anne over. The Queen's life was dull and dreary. Completely neglected by Louis, her husband only in name, and excluded even from formal Court functions by the jealousy of the Queen-Mother, she found that Marie, with her lively conversation and her quick repartee, added gaiety to the empty days and made them seem less boring. Marie on her part felt a deep sympathy for the neglected and visibly suffering young Queen, and a devoted friendship soon sprang up between them. The marriage proposal from Luynes, the most intimate associate of the King, held out every prospect for a still closer bond.

When Marie's father was informed that the King's favourite was doing him the honour of asking for the hand of his daughter, he well understood the motive. The Rohan family belonged to the highest nobility of France, claiming descent from the ancient sovereigns of Brittany before the Roman conquest, but the upstart was the actual ruler of the country and all the nobles were in need of Government favour. The extravagant life of the Court and the luxury that had to be maintained, in spite of the continual rise in prices, had made marriages between the high nobility and members of the despised but rich merchant families quite a common occurrence. Nevertheless, when the marriage contract was drawn up, the Duc de Montbazon made a gesture in accordance with the family's reputation by promising his daughter a dowry of 200,000 livres, a yearly payment of 10,000 livres from her share of her mother's fortune and other benefits, which was all in excess of his means. He had no intention of paying anything; none of the money ever came to her, and after his death, thirty-seven years later, the promise led to court proceedings, but the marriage contract was drawn up as befitted a family of the standing of the Rohans. For Luynes, on his part, such financial matters were of no importance since he had appropriated all the riches which Concini had amassed, and he possessed all he could desire. Marie's charms had actually captured him and he was deeply in love with his young bride.

Thus, five months after the murder of Concini, the marriage of Luynes and Marie de Rohan was solemnized in the Royal Chapel at the Louvre. The Archbishop of Tours, in whose diocese the Château de Couzières, Marie's birth-place, lay, officiated, and the King attended the splendid celebrations. As a wedding present Luynes gave his wife the magnificent jewellery collected by Concini and he also bought for her a palace near the Louvre which he enlarged and re-equipped.

It was not long before Louis, too, found a special pleasure in Marie's company. To his great surprise she knew a great deal about horses, falconry and similar activities that were so near to his heart, which derived from her wild and unfettered childhood on her father's estate, but was nevertheless unusual among ladies of the Court. It delighted the King. In conversation with her, Louis lost his usual reticence, talked freely and vividly and even enjoyed her witty repartee. Soon he began to come for supper regularly at Luynes' apartments, so providing a new subject for Court gossip. But Marie managed to dispel Anne's initial jealousy, particularly when, thanks to her efforts, Louis started to invite both ladies to his beloved hunting parties, which were already a pleasant change in Anne's dull life.

Sixteen months after the marriage Marie gave birth to a daughter and now, when she had just reached the age of eighteen, Louis appointed her 'Superintendent of the Queen's Household and Purse and Head of Her Council', a position which gave her precedence and authority over all members of Anne's Court. The appointment provoked a revolt among the old-established Court ladies. Some of them even preferred to resign rather than accept such a young girl as their senior, and the Spanish ladies who had come with Anne to France departed – to the great satisfaction of Louis who declared he had a strong aversion to 'these widows dressed like nuns'. After their departure, according to some reports, Luynes even succeeded in dragging the King out of bed and inducing him for once to sleep with the Queen.

Under Marie's direction Queen Anne's intimate circle changed its character and became a merry gathering at which reigned such frivolity of conversation that the Court gossips were scandalized. The Papal Nuncio induced the Queen's confessor to use his influence with Anne, but his remonstrances made no impression. Even the Duc de Montbazon, who had now been appointed Governor of Paris and of the Ile-de-France, felt it his duty to inform Louis that his daughter had brought to the Queen the notorious *Cabinet Satirique*, full of pornographic verses, for her to read, but the sources do not report whether Marie had found it among her father's books and taken it away. In any case, Anne started to enjoy the gallant conversation and the adoring attitudes of the brilliant and attractive young noblemen whom Marie drew to her circle. Her womanly pride was awakened.

However, this pleasant Court life could not endure for long; outside events interfered. The high nobility, disappointed by Luynes, was only waiting for the right occasion to bring about the fall of the new upstart whom Louis had made a duke and a peer of France. The great feudal nobility, dwelling in their provinces, towns and fortresses, only needed a rallying point to join for open resistance. And it was the Queen-Mother who provided them with the right pretext.

Marie de Medici did not intend to spend her life as a semi-prisoner in the solitude of Blois. In spite of all the spies surrounding her, she managed to make contact with some of the discontented nobles and particularly with the Duc d'Epernon, Governor of Metz and other fortresses in the east as well as some provinces in the west, who, after the assassination of Henri IV, had forced Parlement to recognize her as Regent and who was now prepared to help her again. He left his son, the Marquis de la Valette, in command of Metz; de la Valette closed all gates of the city to prevent any information from leaking out, while the Duke himself rode with some hundred guards through half of France to Angoulême. From there he informed the Queen-Mother that he was waiting for her, and Marie de Medici risked her life, fleeing from Blois in the middle of the night by descending the wall of the fortress on a rope-ladder. D'Epernon soon collected 5,000 foot-soldiers and 800 horsemen and called upon other dissatisfied nobles to join him. Civil war threatened.

After her flight, Marie de Medici had written to her son that she had regained her freedom in order to be able to counsel him in matters of State, the downfall of which she foresaw if it remained in the hands of those at present directing it. The Court, aware of the feeling in the country, was greatly perturbed. To avoid the worst one had to try to negotiate and some ecclesiastics at Court suggested to the King that he recall the Bishop of Luçon, who had once been the Queen-Mother's favourite and always 'counselled moderation and worked in the interest of the Court'.

The Bishopric of Luçon was one of the poorest and most insignificant in France, but the young Bishop, Armand Jean de Richelieu, managed to win the attention of the Queen-Regent at the assembly of the Estates General with a speech full of flattery and praise for her and for her regency. Phrases like 'Happy is the King to whom God has given such a mother', or 'The whole of France regards itself as pledged to give Your Majesty all the honours which in every age have been accorded to the guardians of peace and order and public security', could not fail to make a favourable impression on the mind of Marie de Medici; and when Louis and Anne were married she had appointed the Bishop, then twenty-nine years old, as Almoner to the young Queen. Next year he became private secretary to Marie de Medici herself and Councillor of State.

He was soon employed on various missions to arrange an understanding with some rebels in the provinces and showed great skill in the diplomatic game and in reaching a compromise. However, he was regarded as Concini's man, as some of his letters found after the Italian's death had shown, and he was not further used except to escort the Queen-Mother to Blois. For a while he was allowed to remain there as her confidential counsellor and adviser, but as soon as she was considered under safe guard in the fortress, he had been exiled to the Papal enclave of Avignon, in spite of her protests and complaints. Now that she had escaped from Blois and civil war threatened, the King himself wrote Richelieu a letter, instructing him to proceed with all possible speed to Angoulême and to resume his old position as the Queen's counsellor.

This was a clever move. In spite of the indignant resistance of her present advisers, some of whom even threatened to leave her, Marie de Medici took the return of Richelieu as evidence that her son was sympathetic to her wishes and was trying to satisfy them. Richelieu's advice to her was to come to terms with the King, since her supporters did not possess sufficient power for active resistance, and on being charged to undertake the negotiations he succeeded within a month in concluding the Treaty of Angoulême, which gave her the governorship of the province of Anjou, with its important towns, strongholds and castles, and granted her a royal establishment with the right to engage or dismiss any person as she thought fit. All her allies were pardoned.

Thus it seemed that civil war had been averted, and the country was expecting a visible sign of the reconciliation of the royal family. A meeting between mother and son was to be arranged, but this took longer then negotiating the peace treaty. It took place only after four months of arduous discussion in the Château of Couzières, which belonged to the Duc de Montbazon, and it proved unsatisfactory. Although the Queen-Mother and the King wept and vowed to forget their grievances and remain friends, they had nothing to say to each other and were embarrassed. She felt humiliated because Marie had arranged that on each occasion Queen Anne took precedence over her. Moreover, in the King's entourage she saw Vitry, the man who had killed Concini, now as Marshal of France. All her opponents were present around the King, now in high positions, and when mother and son parted, many of the great nobles also left the Court and went into their provinces to prepare for a new revolt.

An endless exchange of diplomatic notes followed. As Richelieu wrote: 'Luynes entreated the Queen to come to Court, but feared nothing so much as that she might come; the Queen declared that she wished to come to Court, but had no thought of doing so.' Resistance to Luynes was being organized all over the country, and taking into account all the great nobles on her side, the Queen's party appeared to be very powerful; but when, next summer, Louis opened the campaign with his small army, the towns and castles, one after the other, opened their gates to him without a shot, since their interests did not coincide with those of the feudal lords. Finally, a battle at the bridge-head over the Loire at Anger, connecting the north and the south of France, was fought, and the defeat which was inflicted on the undisciplined rebel forces robbed them of all hope of continuing their resistance. Again Richelieu was sent to the King's camp to negotiate a new agreement, and the rebellious nobility was very much afraid of what the new terms would be.

To their delight, Richelieu returned after a few days with an agreement which confirmed all the clauses of the Treaty of Angoulême, again with full amnesty for the Queen's supporters, while she herself had only to promise to live in peace and on good terms with the Court. To achieve these unexpected results Richelieu cleverly played on the fears of Luynes. The upstart knew that he could never be sure of his followers. If they saw an advantage somewhere, they would at any moment change sides. He also understood that public opinion held him responsible for the division between the King and the Queen-Mother and therefore for all the damage it had done the country. Moreover, there was a lot of talk that the Huguenots might unite forces and join the Queen; Richelieu played on this fear and suggested that, if peace were concluded, many Catholic recruits from the rebel forces would join the royal army. Harsh conditions would only intensify the hatred – and Luynes gave in. Again a meeting between the King and his mother was to be arranged, but when it took place in August 1620, nearly a whole year after the first one, it brought disappointment to Richelieu. He had expected a seat in the King's Council as recognition of his services; however, Louis only agreed, at his mother's request, to apply to the Pope for a cardinal's hat for him.

With this reconciliation achieved, Luynes hoped to return to Paris, but there he encountered the King's resistance. Louis had found army life to his taste. He was continually reminded by the clergy of the fact that already his father, Henri IV, had promised the Catholic bishops of Béarn the restitution of the Church property which had been confiscated by the Huguenots, and he decided to fulfil the promise. He now had his troops at hand in the south and so he invaded Béarn. The province was well prepared for defence, but neither its nobility nor its towns had believed that the King would undertake such an action, and when he suddenly appeared with his army, he met scarcely any resistance. The provincial Protestant government was dissolved, the Huguenot militia disbanded and new garrisons installed everywhere. The Church property was retaken and a Catholic regent appointed.

After this rapid and complete success the King and his favourite returned to Paris, but not for long. Strong winter gales had damaged the fortifications in the harbour of Calais, and Louis went there with Luynes to inspect the damage. While they were in Calais, at Christmas 1620, Marie gave birth to a boy in Paris. When the messenger reached Calais, the King was the first to receive the news, and he ordered the guns of the citadel to be discharged and then embraced his favourite, who came in all haste to enquire about the meaning of the salvo, and was told that he had a son. After their return to Paris the King paid a hurried visit to Anne and then rushed to Marie's apartments, kissed the baby and later stood godfather to the child. The christening service was performed with the same rites as for royal children.

Outwardly the splendid Court life of Paris was resumed, but slowly the courtiers became aware of a change in the King's attitude to Luynes. The excessive display, in which his favourite indulged, annoyed him. On one occasion, when he saw Luynes passing before his windows with a magnificent retinue, Louis remarked, 'There goes King Luynes!' Thus a typical trait in Louis' character became apparent: he could not tolerate anyone behaving as if he had any power or position except insofar as it was granted him by the King's pleasure.

Nevertheless, he still needed Luynes, as he knew no one whom he could sufficiently trust to replace him, and he even made him Constable of France, for a new campaign was due to begin. Warned by last year's example in Béarn, the Huguenots were rearming everywhere. So, when summer came, the royal army set out once more to the south; but this time the defence was organized and a fierce campaign of sieges began. The countryside was ravaged; frightful atrocities were committed in captured strongholds; but while the King bravely dared to expose himself to danger in battle, Luynes always conspicuously chose some safe point of observation out of the range of fire.

The attitude of the Constable provided food for gossip. Sarcastic, scurrilous pamphlets came flooding in from Paris, while Louis himself was not sparing with sneering remarks. When in addition the news of the latest Court scandal arrived in camp, which intimated that, in Paris, Marie had taken advantage of her husband's absence to start a love affair with the Duc de Chevreuse, Louis, before all the courtiers, told the Constable that he had better take care. Afterwards, one of the King's clergymen remonstrated with him saying that it was considered a sin to sow dissension between husband and wife; the reply he received was that Louis hoped God would forgive him, but he had not been able to resist the temptation to revenge himself on Marie and to annoy the Constable.

Now his dissatisfaction with Luynes was aggravated by a grudge against Marie, because of the changes which she had made in the Queen's Court and, he believed, even in the character of Anne herself. He found that the young Queen was no longer as shy and demure as she had been, but now showed a less restrained behaviour and a will of her own; and Marie's free and easy attitude and glib wit simply lacked due respect. When the Huguenot fortress of Montauban proved impregnable to the attack and the army settled down for a prolonged siege, the ladies sometimes came to visit the camp and the arrangement was that they were to leave it before nightfall. Once they stayed until after dark, and when Louis objected to their sleeping in the camp, as there were no beds available, Marie called out, 'Surely the King has a bed,' and ran laughing out of the room. Such behaviour infuriated the King, now twenty-one years old, and although he said nothing the discontent welled up within him.

All efforts against Montauban were in vain and, when winter approached, it became apparent that, expecting a war of short duration, Luynes had failed to provide adequate equipment for the needs of the troops, and the siege had to be lifted. He was not unaware of the strong feeling against him and did not dare to return to Paris before showing some measure of success; and so he attacked the small castle of Montheurt. But now all manner of disease broke out among the badly provisioned troops, and Luynes himself fell ill. Two days after the fall of the castle, while it was being razed to the ground, he died of scarlet fever in his forty-fourth year, on December 15, 1621, after four years of splendour as the most powerful man in the land.

His death was immediately exploited by all. On the way back to Paris, already in Orléans, Louis was met by Richelieu, and Richelieu spared no efforts in trying to convince the King that the Queen-Mother should again be given a voice in the Royal Council. She now lived in the newly built Palais du Luxembourg, and in her letters about the state of affairs in Paris and in the country she had lately given ample proof of her concern and of her grasp of political problems. When as a result of Richelieu's efforts the meeting of the King and his mother took place, the understanding between them was so good that the Apostolic Nuncio reported to Rome that Richelieu was the only man who had the ability to manage both mother and son; accordingly he was soon created a Cardinal.

Louis' first action after his return was to dismiss all Luynes' relatives from Court. Marie was ordered to move from the Louvre, but according to the rules the Superintendent of the Queen's Court had to reside in the Palace, and so she was only forced to exchange her luxurious apartments near the Queen for some simple rooms in a wing, in spite of the fact that she was expecting her confinement any day. And when she gave birth to a daughter Louis did not even consider it necessary to congratulate her. But his attitude in no way affected the close relationship between Anne and her. On the contrary, as the first activity of the Queen-Mother was to stir up Louis against his wife in order to bring him again under her own exclusive influence, Marie's friendship now became Anne's sole consolation. It was to Marie alone she could turn with all her sorrows, and to cheer up her friend, who was now pregnant, and notwithstanding her recent widowhood, Marie arranged more and more amusing entertainments at which the conversation sometimes became so frivolous that it especially scandalized the clergymen, who tried in vain to remind the Queen of the propriety expected of her. Undeterred, Marie introduced further brilliant young courtiers into the Queen's circle, who paid her homage and flattered her vanity.

It was after one such gathering that in a romp with Marie and another of her ladies through the Grande Salle of the Louvre

Anne stumbled and fell. Two days later she had a miscarriage. Louis was in Orléans at the time, and when the news reached him he summarily dismissed Marie from the Queen's service, ordered her immediate removal from the Louvre and instructed Anne to sever all connections. At first the Queen refused to obey. She demanded an explanation as to the faults Marie had committed so that she herself might punish her, but the King only repeated his instruction. There was a great exchange of messengers, but all complaints and supplications were in vain. Louis remained adamant and the only concession which Anne obtained was the permission to see her friend from time to time, but 'only very rarely'.

Thus, four months after the death of Luynes, Marie was expelled from Court and deprived of any real contact with her friend whose well-being had been her main concern for so long.

Chapter II

Marie's banishment was for Anne an even worse blow than for Marie herself. It was generally recognized that the Queen's greatest solace was the concern with which Marie participated in all her sorrows and misfortunes, and now she had nobody to whom she could go and confide her troubles, knowing she would receive consolation. She was in despair and wept. Marie's reaction was entirely different. She was furious, and her fury made her blood boil. She was a Rohan and the motto of the house of Rohan was *Roi ne puis, prince ne daigne, Rohan je suis!* No power could intimidate her, and she would prove her spirit to them.

Three days after her removal from the Louvre her plan was ready. She wrote to the man who had been her lover, Claude de Lorraine, Duc de Chevreuse, describing the misfortune that had overtaken her and asking him to marry her.

Claude's position at Court was a singular one: as a prince of the House of Lorraine he was not a French subject, but as the Duc de Chevreuse, without ceasing to be a foreigner, he had a position in the French aristocracy in line with his rank. He held the office of Grand Chamberlain and had luxurious apartments in the Louvre, just above those of the King. Through his sister the Princesse de Conti, he was related to the royal family: Marie de Medici called him 'my nephew'. When he went abroad he was received with the honour accorded to members of quasi-sovereign houses.

When Marie's letter was brought to him by her messenger, as he happened to be absent from Paris, he had a long consultation with some of his friends and in the end decided that he would fail in his duty to the King if he married a person so disliked by His Majesty. But when he came back to Paris he was incautious enough to visit Marie and fell again under the spell of her beauty and her wit. To overcome his last resistance, she promised to write herself to the King to solicit his permission of the marriage and timed the letter precisely so that Louis received it after the wedding ceremony, held privately and secretly, had been performed. It took place less than five months after the death of Luynes.

When Louis received the letter he was furious and wanted to refuse his consent, but as the marriage had already taken place, he was forced, in accordance with etiquette, to send instead a letter of congratulation which arrived when the couple were on their honeymoon, visiting their various châteaux and far-flung domains. Marie visited every village and hamlet and was everywhere enthusiastically welcomed. She was particularly enchanted by the Château de Dampierre, situated in the valley of the river Ivette; and as it was so near to Paris she chose it as her country retreat. Her husband promised to provide it with a park, with gardens, ponds and fountains in accordance with the most elegant fashion of the time. He did it in a lordly manner, simply by fencing in adjoining pieces of land wherever it seemed desirable.

The King's letter of congratulation did not contain a single word about Marie's readmission to Court. That meant that she was still banished and the Louvre remained closed to her. When the newly married couple returned to Paris, they took up residence in the palace which Luynes had bought for Marie and which henceforth became known as the Hôtel de Chevreuse. The Duc de Chevreuse, a brave soldier, forty-five years old, was, as not unusual in those days, also a reckless spender, always short of cash and deeply in debt, and the share of the riches of Luynes which had passed to Marie was a welcome contribution to their luxurious way of life. But the most important task now was to secure Marie's reinstatement.

Louis was still on his campaign against the Huguenots in Guyenne, and Chevreuse joined him there, distinguishing himself again by his bravery; he was therefore made a member of the Council of War. Nevertheless, it took him six weeks of patient, careful effort before he obtained permission from the King for Marie to come back to Court, and that only after Louis had taken care to abolish the office of Superintendent of the Queen's Household, previously held by Marie, so that she would no longer have any official position or duties to fulfil.

Nevertheless, it was a victory for the 22-year-old Marie de Rohan, achieved over all her adversaries and over the King himself. Now no longer merely the wife of a favourite of the King, but a member of a foreign royal house, she had the right to the address 'Madame' followed by the name of her husband's duchy, and it is as Mme de Chevreuse that Marie de Rohan entered into the history of France as one of the most fascinating, but at the same time one of the most controversial and most hated, among French political women.

At the time nobody could foresee such a development. Her reappearance at Court was simply seen as the return of the Queen's best-loved and trusted friend, and although the royal duties and services of honour which she had previously performed had been taken away from her, the intimate relationship between the Queen and herself was immediately re-established, and the two were again inseparable. Meanwhile Louis was still waging his campaign against the Huguenots, which turned out as unsuccessful as the first one under Luynes. When, after long bargaining, the Peace Treaty of Montepellier was signed in October 1622, it confirmed the Edict of Nantes which gave the Huguenots religious freedom, and in addition bestowed governorships and pensions upon their leaders, among whom were Henri de Rohan and his brother Soubise, relatives of Marie.

The winter after Louis' return was a dismal one. Plague broke out in Paris, and people at Court preferred to flee, some to St Germain and others to Fontainebleau. The King spent more and more time in the company of his mother, who spared no effort to regain her former influence over him, hoping thus to recover her dominant position in the Government. This augured a fresh campaign against Anne, whom she accused of disrespect. There were constant quarrels between the two queens about questions of precedence, and accusations of encroachment upon each other's privileges. When the Court eventually returned to Paris the Queen-Mother persuaded Louis to transfer State receptions from the Louvre to her Palais du Luxembourg, and she made sure that Anne was not invited, saying that through her inexperience she 'might spoil the ceremonial'. It was certainly under Marie's influence that Anne responded to this treatment by making her apartments in the Louvre a centre of all kinds of lighthearted entertainment with impromptu masquerades and ballets, brilliant amusements and much laughter. Louis tartly reprimanded his wife about the frivolous atmosphere at her Court, but Anne now proved her new self-assurance and retorted angrily. Relations between the royal couple deteriorated.

Later, Richelieu accused Marie in his memoirs:

'She has been the ruin of the Queen, whose natural healthy intelligence she led astray by her bad example; she dominated the heart of the Queen, spoiled her, made her neglect her duty to the King and brought about the complete estrangement of the royal couple.'

What Richelieu overlooked in his assessment was the real cause of this estrangement. As Mme de Motteville, one of Anne's most devoted and trusted adherents, put it:

'The Queen's misfortune was that the King, her husband, did not love her enough and that she therefore felt herself bound to occupy her feelings otherwise and give her affection to the ladies who misused the favour. Instead of inducing the Queen in the early years to behave more according to her husband's wishes and to try to win his love, they sought on the contrary to make her withdraw from him more and more.'

About this time, in March 1623, two distinguished Englishmen appeared in Paris on their way to Spain. They naturally travelled incognito, and according to custom the incognito was strictly preserved. Nevertheless they were given access to the entertainments of the Court, had the opportunity to see the Queen with nineteen of her ladies dancing in a masque and a ballet, and were delighted. These strangers were Charles, Prince of Wales, and Lord Buckingham.

The reason for their journey was the intended marriage of the Prince of Wales and the Spanish Infanta, and it had been Buckingham's idea that they should go to Spain and conduct the negotiations personally. The enterprise was a failure; the political and religious obstacles were too great. Moreover, Buckingham's personal behaviour offended Spanish susceptibilities in matters of etiquette. In England itself the feeling against this marriage was shown by the enthusiastic rejoicing in London on the return of the two travellers after nearly eight months' absence without reaching an agreement with the Spaniards. Thus the idea of the Spanish marriage was replaced by an alternative plan that Charles should marry the fifteen-year-old sister of Louis XIII, Henriette-Marie. Two English envoys were sent to Paris, informally of course, to investigate the position. As their mission, too, was unofficial they could not be formally entertained in the Louvre and became the daily guests of the Duc de Chevreuse.

The Duc de Chevreuse was eager to promote this marriage. Through his great-aunt, Mary of Guise, wife of King James V of Scotland, he was related to the English royal house of Stuart and acted with pleasure the part of an unofficial go-between. At this time his own marriage had assumed the conventional pattern of the period, as was the custom with the aristocracy: with the riches of Luynes at his disposal the Duke resumed his old love affairs with various beautiful ladies at the Court, and when the scandalmongers tried to provoke Marie, she cut them short with the remark that she could well cope with the situation. She now spent much of her time in the company of the leading English envoy, Lord Holland, who was considered to be one of the most handsome men in the world, although his face and features looked more like those of a very beautiful woman – a peculiarity which had gained him the affections of James I of England and laid him open to his monarch's caresses. Here in Paris and in constant touch with Marie, he fell in love with her and she with him.

Naturally his mission had to be a complete success, and she volunteered to guide him. At first he had to pay homage to the Queen-Mother, then to Anne, who felt offended because of the slight to her sister, the Infanta, and whose agreement to the French marriage Marie had first to obtain. Then the intended bride was to be persuaded to look favourably upon the portrait of Charles and the prospect of the English throne; and the letters to London were full of praise of Henriette-Marie's charms.

But now a new influence was making itself increasingly felt at the French Court as well as in the Government: that of Richelieu. On the insistent pressure of the Queen-Mother, Louis had at last given way and appointed him to the Royal Council, and immediately all Richelieu's energies were directed towards winning the King's confidence. In his relation with the other ministers he claimed precedence on account of his rank as Cardinal, but in his behaviour to Louis he displayed humility, maintaining that he had only accepted the burden of the new position, disregarding his uncertain health, out of obedience and because of his desire to serve the King. He had completely summed up the King's character and made it a rule always to act in accordance therewith.

Louis, who in his childhood had not been able to offer resistance to the ill-treatment to which he was subjected, had developed a hatred against anything that could be regarded as an attempt to impose somebody else's will upon him or even merely to influence him. The simplest advice about how to act was sufficient to make him do the contrary. Any show of independent action by anyone made him furious. Any sign of self-assertion led to disgrace. Being a weak man, he endeavoured to uphold the majesty of the crown by demanding a completely submissive attitude from everyone around him; and Richelieu played up to the King's foibles. In the Royal Council he did not speak of his own accord but waited for the Queen-Mother to ask for his opinion. She did this during the discussion about Henriette-Marie's marriage. The First Minister to whose position he aspired, had expressed himself against the marriage, so Richelieu therefore brought forward all the advantages which an English alliance could bring, stressing, however, the necessity of careful negotiations to secure freedom of worship for the English Catholics and settlement also of other considerations. It was during these prolonged negotiations that he really achieved his aim of becoming the King's First Minister. When all the marriage clauses were agreed and the contract had been signed it was already late autumn, and so it was decided that the marriage ceremony should take place in the following spring, in May 1625.

Charles intended to come to Paris himself, but the death of his father James I and his own coronation made it impossible for him to leave England. A proxy had to be chosen and the person on whom the honour fell to represent the King of England at the marriage ceremony was the Duc de Chevreuse.

After the formal marriage ceremony on the platform erected in front of Notre Dame, the procession, headed by Louis, entered the cathedral to hear Mass, while the Duc de Chevreuse, as the proxy for the Protestant King, remained outside in the cloisters accompanied by the English envoys. At the splendid State banquet in the evening the personages sitting with the King, the Queen-Mother, Queen Anne and Henriette-Marie, now Queen of England, were the Duc de Chevreuse and the English envoys. And the only woman not a queen to be seated at this royal table, served by the highest nobility of the land, was Marie de Rohan, Mme de Chevreuse.

Buckingham had planned to come to Paris for the marriage in person, so that he could be acclaimed for having achieved the link between the two royal houses, but being delayed by affairs in England he could only arrive thirteen days later. Ostensibly he was to escort Henriette-Marie to her royal husband, but in reality he was there to persuade Louis and Richelieu to enter into an alliance to take common action with regard to Spain and affairs in Germany, where the Emperor's religious war against the Protestant states was assuming dangerous proportions.

Buckingham's plan to come to Paris gave Marie and Holland the idea to prepare the ground for a romantic attachment between him and Anne. The fascinating personality and superb physique of this 'best-looking man in the world' was meant to awaken tender feelings in the frustrated young Queen, who, as Marie's confidante, knew everything about Marie's own love affair with Holland and found the liaison very entertaining. As Buckingham's friend, Holland missed no opportunity to praise him to Anne, describing his brilliance, his passionate personality and his remarkable wit, and Marie, too, talked of him perpetually.

Now, two weeks after the marriage of Henriette-Marie, 'he [Buckingham] appeared at Court with so much splendour that he filled the populace with admiration, the ladies with delight, the gallants with jealousy and the husbands with a feeling worse than that'. He was formally received by Louis and the Queen-Mother with great pomp, but Anne, again practically confined to her own apartments in the Louvre, could only receive him in an unofficial audience when he came to pay her homage. Yet from the very first meeting there was an understanding between them 'as if they had known each other for a long time'. She was naturally thrilled that this romantic man had, as he asserted, loved her in secret for two long years, ever since he had once seen her dancing on the occasion of his previous unofficial visit; and the joy of being so admired could not have failed to stir her. On his part the idea of adding a queen to his innumerable amorous conquests must have intrigued him. In any case their friendly understanding and informal conversation with each other immediately became the subject of gossip.

After a week of sojourn, filled with festivities and entertainments, the task of conducting the young Queen of England to her new country had to be undertaken in spite of Buckingham's failure to win the King's or Richelieu's agreement to his political plans. On French soil the whole Court, a cavalcade of about 4,000 persons, was to accompany Henriette-Marie on her journey to the coast. Louis himself felt unwell because of a cold and remained in Fontainebleau. The other travellers split into groups and, escorted by detachments of guards and their attendants, took different routes to Boulogne. After travelling for five days the solemn entry into Amiens took place with royal homage and was followed by balls and banquets. The Queen-Mother and Henriette-Marie were lodged in the episcopal palace, while a luxurious house with a large garden in the vicinity had been assigned to Anne and her suite. Then the Queen-Mother suddenly fell ill and retired to bed, whereupon Henriette-Marie refused to continue the journey until her mother had recovered. During this time Anne received daily visits from Buckingham and Holland who always came officially to see the Duchesse de Chevreuse.

Once, at dusk, they were all walking in the garden, with the Queen's attendants remaining at a discreet distance and out of sight, and Marie and Holland purposely fell behind to leave Anne and Buckingham alone together on the path, when suddenly a shrill scream from Anne shattered the quiet of the evening. At once the chamberlain rushed forward with drawn sword, and the attendants, with Marie and Holland in the forefront, hurried to the spot, where they found Anne sobbing and Buckingham kneeling at her feet and begging forgiveness. According to La Porte, a devoted member of Anne's household, 'he had taken the insolent liberty of attempting to kiss the Queen'. She was now being led indoors by Marie and the other ladies, whilst Buckingham and Holland quickly disappeared. Next day the Queen-Mother ordered Henriette-Marie to resume her journey to the coast immediately, and Anne managed to convince her mother-in-law that she had been the innocent victim of an unprovoked attack.

When the news of the incident reached Louis, he refused to believe in Anne's innocence, banned all the male attendants who had accompanied her to Amiens from Court and decided that Buckingham should never again enter France. Mme de Chevreuse, however, was by then outside his jurisdiction, for despite her advanced state of pregnancy she had prevailed upon her husband to take her with him to England.

In London the plague was raging, and Charles retired with his young Queen to Hampton Court and assigned to the Duc and Duchesse de Chevreuse lodgings in Richmond Palace, with Denmark House as a town residence. Just as Buckingham had dazzled the French Court, so did Marie and her husband fill the English Court with delight and admiration. The Duchess sparkled with diamonds and wit; the Duke always appeared in a kind of a sedan-chair carried by 'mules covered with the most splendid trappings ever seen', and the 24-year-old Marie turned the heads of all the gallants at the Court. Lord Holland was always at her side, Buckingham paid her frequent visits, and soon the three formed a very cheerful trio. Her gaiety and her high spirits in spite of her condition enchanted everybody and scandalized particularly the clerics who had accompanied the Queen.

As the other ladies followed her lead, the Bishop of Mende, Richelieu's cousin, wrote to the Cardinal, 'It looks as if these ladies had come over to establish brothels rather than to serve religion!' and he complained that Mme de Chevreuse and another lady had had long talks with a Protestant pastor and that they ate meat in public on fast-days. He considered that it would be best if Marie were at once recalled to France, but when Louis ordered her to return, he received from King Charles the reply that in her condition she was unfit to undertake such a journey and that he insisted on keeping her in England until after the awaited birth. Buckingham as well as Holland offered her their houses for the confinement, but finally she was brought to bed at Hampton Court and there gave birth to a daughter. A couple of weeks later she shocked the French ambassador and some puritanical English people by swimming across the Thames!

But now there could no longer be any excuse for disobeying the repeated orders from Louis to return to Paris, and the Duke and the Duchess embarked on the journey home, although Marie had her misgivings. Nevertheless, except for a few caustic remarks, the reception at Court was not uncordial, because there had arrived at the same time an enthusiastic letter from King Charles to Louis thanking him 'for so singular a favour and also for the wisdom with which You made Your choice of a person in whom We have found so much cause for content and satisfaction'. And after expressing his admiration for Marie he appealed to Louis to show him the kindness of assisting him to render her the thanks he owed her for the 'great honour and felicity which We have received through her. She returns to You worthy to be a shining star of any court and the precious proof of Our mutual friendship.'

With such a letter in his hands Louis was again prevented from venting his anger on Marie, but as always he let it fester in his mind, and his animosity against her became even stronger. Richelieu as usual acted diplomatically and showed great friendliness towards her, so that she reported it to London, whereupon he received a letter from Lord Holland thanking him, mentioning that 'His Majesty and the Queen were very pleased to hear of your kindness to Mme de Chevreuse', and concluding his letter with high praises of her.

Thus Marie did not need to have any fears for herself, but she knew precisely what had been going on in Paris, as she had been in continuous correspondence with Anne and was not surprised to find the Queen in a very dejected mood. Deprived of loyal attendants upon whom she could depend, she was in a most humiliating position. Her degradation went so far that she was not even permitted to leave the palace premises without special permission from the King, whom she saw only on formal State occasions. The Queen-Mother and her favourite Richelieu dominated the scene, whilst Richelieu, in pursuance of his policy, continued to display humility before the King, purporting to give advice only when asked and offering his resignation continually, knowing that it would not be accepted. In this way he got rid of all ministers who might be his opponents and replaced them by his own men. His rule was felt to be even more oppressive than that of Concini and the later oppression of Luynes, because, while they had bribed the opposing nobles with money, concessions or appointments, Richelieu's actions were intended to suppress them completely. He even issued an edict ordering the demolition of fortifications situated elsewhere than at the frontiers, with the aim of depriving the nobles of centres of resistance which they could use in case of open strife. The prevailing mood was one of conspiracy and rebellion and it needed only some minor incident to spark off a revolt.

The provocation came with the announcement by the Queen-Mother that her second son Gaston, now a youth of seventeen, was going to marry the Princesse de Montpensier. The Princess belonged to a branch of the Bourbon family and was the richest heiress in France, the owner of half a dozen duchies and of enormous domains. This declaration enraged the other members of the royal house. Louis had always been of very delicate and uncertain health, he could die at any time and the greatest families of the country had for a long time secretly cherished the hope that one day the crown could be theirs. It was known that the Duc de Vendôme, also a son of Henri IV but by Gabrielle d'Estrées, had declared that illegitimate children could accede to the throne equally well as legitimate offspring. The Comte de Soissons on the other hand, also a Bourbon, had himself intended to marry Mlle de Montpensier.

But worst hit of all by the idea of Gaston's marriage was Anne. If Gaston married and had children, what would become of her? Gaston was a vacillating, unreliable person, spoilt and weak, and would always be a puppet in the hands of his mother, whose darling he was. If Louis died, he would nominally be King and in practice Marie de Medici would again be Regent and actual ruler. That meant that Anne would be banished to some distant retreat on a meagre pension without any hope for the future. Marie was fully aware of the danger to her friend and had at the first rumours of the intended marriage developed a plan as to how to avert it: Gaston had to be induced to refuse to marry Mlle de Montpensier and to retain his freedom, so that if Louis died he could marry Anne, who would then become the real Queen. It has not been established whether the idea reached the ear of Anne herself, but anyway Marie set to work to put it into practice.

The main problem was to find someone who could guide Gaston along the way mapped out for him. The man who had the greatest influence on him was the superintendent of his household and head of his council, the old Marshal of France d'Ornano, and Marie was still on the friendly terms established with him in the times of Luynes, whose adherent he had been. She also knew that his ambitions were being thwarted by Richelieu, who had refused his request to attend the Council of State at Gaston's side, and with the help of some other ladies of high rank in Anne's circle she set out to win him over.

The idea to be implanted in Gaston's mind was that by marrying a subject of the King he would lower his own standing, since his fortune and his lands would always remain in his brother's power. It was pointed out that there were so many princesses of foreign ruling houses whom he could marry and then, in case of need, he would be able to count on the support and help of other sovereigns. Moreover, he was very fond of Anne, and if Louis should die she would be free, and if he wanted he could then marry her. So he refused the proposed marriage, declaring that it was not because of any aversion to the proposed bride but because he did not want to bind himself.

Naturally the cabal against the marriage was only of small importance compared with the aim to overthrow Richelieu's government. All the nobles of high rank had the same desire and promised help and action: the Prince de Condé, the Comte de Soissons, the Duc de Vendôme and his brother the Grand Prior of France, the Duc de Longueville, all were prepared to raise troops in their provinces, to provide money and to rise up in revolt everywhere. Gaston was to demand the dismissal of Richelieu, and if he failed, he was to leave the Court, retire to Dieppe, Le Havre, Sedan or Metz, all safe towns in the hands of the rebels, and take up arms. They even opened negotiations with foreign governments: with Savoy, England, Spain, Holland; they all were sympathetic, and some promised help.

Richelieu's spies were naturally active, but they could not report anything more than rumours to the effect that some plot was in the offing and signs of unusual activity around Gaston and Ornano. When after Easter 1626 the Court moved to Fontainebleau, Richelieu induced Louis to invite Ornano to dinner. This was followed by an inspection of a regiment of guards which he had summoned to Fontainebleau, and then the Marshal was arrested.

The sudden, unexpected arrest of Ornano was a crushing blow to the conspirators. Gaston's demand for his release fell on deaf ears. Not only did the King disregard it but also the Queen-Mother, who realized that the refusal of her usually obedient son to marry Mlle de Montpensier was the result of Ornano's advice.

Now the grandees expected Gaston to withdraw to one of the fortified towns offered to him and to demand the release of Ornano, backing up his request with arms, but he shrank from such an irrevocable step and so the circle of conspirators persuaded him to make the only possible alternative move: to get rid of Richelieu. Under the pretence of a desire for reconciliation Gaston was to invite himself to a luncheon at Richelieu's country-house at Fleury, but to arrive accompanied by a strong group of his friends and to proceed to make the Cardinal their prisoner, in order to hold him in exchange for Ornano, or, in the scuffle which would certainly ensue, as some hoped, to get rid of him.

Among Gaston's advisers was the Comte de Chalais, who as the Master of the King's Wardrobe was in close contact with Louis yet at the same time professed devotion to Gaston. Moreover, the young man felt a deep love for Marie, whose beauty and wit he admired, and whenever he could he sought to be near her. Thus, after Ornano's arrest, she thought it safe to use him as the go-between with Gaston. Although he was involved in the conspiracy against Richelieu, just before the execution of the plot he was incautious enough to brag about it to a friend, who, under the threat of denouncing the conspiracy, forced him to disclose it to the Cardinal. Richelieu promised Chalais a long-coveted post of colonel in the cavalry, and immediately informed the King, who at once despatched a troop of horse to Fleury. When at dawn Gaston's friends arrived, ostensibly to assist in the preparation for the Prince's visit, Richelieu welcomed them, then drove in his coach to Fontainebleau, professing that he was going to escort His Royal Highness himself to Fleury. Finding Gaston still in bed, he performed the courtesy of handing the Prince his shirt with the remark: 'Monsieur, you have not risen early enough this morning; you will find your quarry is no longer at home.'

The plot was betrayed and Gaston took fright. When interrogated by Richelieu, always in the presence of Louis and the Queen-Mother, he displayed a submissive attitude and betrayed his friends. He even signed a pledge that he would inform his brother of any move or hint of a move directed against the King or his advisers which came to his knowledge. Now there were two traitors among the conspirators, each not sure just how far the other had committed himself, but both maintaining that the revolt should go on and assuring each other of their loyalty and devotion. When Gaston complained to Chalais about the promise which he had been forced to make, Chalais replied that the pledge extorted from him by Richelieu was shameful; he continued to impress on Gaston that it would be dishonourable to leave Ornano to his fate.

Meanwhile, Marie had quickly discovered that there was some kind of connection between Chalais and Richelieu, but counting on his infatuation, and seeing him continually in contact with Gaston as before, she did not cease to trust him. When she heard of their discussions and their irresolution, she recognized that safety now lay only in flight and recommended that they should flee to the eastern provinces, from whence they could in case of need escape to a neighbouring country. Chalais wrote to the governors of Sedan and Metz, while continuing to devise various plans with Gaston.

The Duc de Vendôme had offered the Prince a refuge in Brittany, his domain, where he was secretly arming. However, Richelieu's spies had become aware of the Duke's secret military preparations and Louis set out with the whole Court to Brittany. When he reached Blois it was the official duty of the Duc de Vendôme to come and pay homage to the sovereign on the outskirts of his territory, otherwise he would have had to proclaim an open revolt. His brother, the Grand Prior, had been warned by Marie of the danger to the Duke if he came to Court, and so he tried to obtain from Louis an assurance of his brother's safety. The King's reply was: 'I give you my word that he will come to no more harm than you.' They were both, as sons of Henri IV by Gabrielle d'Estrées, natural brothers of Louis and could not believe that the King would take action against his own brothers; and so they ventured to come. They were graciously received and fêted, but next morning, still in their beds, they were arrested and imprisoned in the Château d'Amboise. When Richelieu demanded that action should be taken against the King's brothers, he had first asked for permission to retire from his post because of failing health, and when Louis, as usual, declined to accept the resignation and reassured him of his support in all his enterprises, the Cardinal carefully instructed the Chief of Police to see to it that the reporters should neither praise nor criticize the acts of the Government but should refrain from mentioning them at all.

Under the prevailing circumstances, only immediate flight could save Gaston and Chalais, but from Blois they would have to ride through the whole of France and the problem was how to avoid being caught while escaping. The long nocturnal visits of Chalais to Gaston's apartments had not remained undetected, and Richelieu ordered the arrest of Chalais.

All these blows had followed one another at incredible speed. Ornano was arrested on May 4th; Chalais' information was given to Richelieu on the 10th; Gaston, after all the interrogations, gave his pledge on the 31st; the Vendômes were arrested on June 12th, and Chalais on July 9th. Now Gaston was completely crushed and said anything that was required of him, accusing everybody: Ornano, Vendôme, Soissons, making damning statements that Queen Anne had advised him to reject the marriage unless Ornano was set free, that Mme de Chevreuse had long ago suggested to him that he should remain unmarried, so that he would eventually be able to marry Anne in case of Louis' death. He finally declared himself ready and willing to marry Mlle de Montpensier as the Queen-Mother wished. The Court had now proceeded to Nantes, and Mlle de Montpensier was ordered to do the same.

Chalais in his dungeon begged Richelieu's and Louis' forgiveness, spoke against all his previous friends, and promised the most devoted and loyal service in future. In his solitude and despair he wrote incessant love-letters to Marie, imploring her to answer him. As she knew that his letters as well as any reply from her would inevitably pass through Richelieu's hands, she made no response. She merely asked his brother to tell him that she could not write, but would do whatever she could to help him. Nevertheless, stung by her silence, he began to pour out hateful accusations against her during his questioning. It was she, he said, who had been the centre of the conspiracy; it was she who had brought all the nobles of high rank together; it was she who had conducted negotiations with the Huguenots through her relatives, the Rohans; it was she who had planned the assassination of Richelieu and incited Gaston to take up arms against the King.

In the meantime Louis, doubting how far the judges could be trusted to find Chalais guilty, on Richelieu's demand created a new authority, a special Court of Criminal Justice to which only the most reliable ministerial and parliamentary councillors were appointed. Marie immediately recognized the purpose of this special court and decided to fulfil her pledge to help Chalais as far as she could. She went personally to Richelieu to ask for mercy for the boy who, in his ignorance, did not understand what he had done. Richelieu listened silently to what she had to say and then simply showed her the accusations which Chalais had made against her. She was aghast. In his letters to her he had written:

'Since my life depends on you, I fear not to hazard it for you, in order to make you understand that I love you. Accept then this little testimony and do not condemn my temerity. If those beautiful eyes that I adore look upon this letter, I augur well for my fortune; but if they do not, I no longer desire my liberty, because in it I shall find my punishment.'

And at the same time he wrote to the Cardinal: 'The whole conversation of this lady consists in telling dissolute stories, bad jokes and execrations.' Entrusting his letter to her to his servant he wrote:

'I begin to learn that one must serve you as a goddess, since I am not permitted to give you any proof of my love without endangering my life. Please protect it therefore, because it is completely dedicated to you alone, and if you esteem it worthy of being preserved, tell this trusted companion of my misfortune that you will sometimes remember the most loving of all men.'

Simultaneously, he wrote to the Cardinal that she had done everything to entice him and tried to awaken his jealousy and to make him abandon the service of the Cardinal by pretending that Richelieu was also in love with her and thus his rival. He even offered to spy upon Mme de Chevreuse and the Queen, just as he had already promised to spy upon Gaston.

Completely stupefied Marie left the Cardinal, and recognizing that her presence at Court would only endanger Anne, she left Nantes and travelled to her retreat at Dampierre.

Now the fate of Chalais, whose breach of confidence had saved the life of Richelieu, was sealed. This Court of Criminal Justice now and in future, when it was summoned for the political trial of dangerous nobles, knew only one sentence: death. But in this case, when the sentence of death was pronounced, it produced an unexpected reversal in Chalais' testimony. He declared before the judges that all the imputations which he had made against Mme de Chevreuse and Queen Anne were lies, invented by him in the hope of saving his own life. Whenever the prosecutor tried to shake his testimony he remained firm. He even sent for his confessor and during his last confession charged the priest to inform the King that everything he had said involving the Queen and Mme de Chevreuse was entirely false.

A week before the execution of Chalais, Ornano died in his prison, and his death created quite a furore. The anticipated trial of Ornano would have meant the questioning of Gaston, the heir presumptive to the throne, who had just been married to the Princesse de Montpensier, with Richelieu himself performing the wedding ceremony. As this marriage was at the root of the whole conspiracy, the confrontation of Gaston with the accused could have become extremely embarrassing. Moreover, the trial would have meant drawing the Queen into public proceedings, dealing not only with the greatest nobles in France but also including ambassadors and possibly foreign governments. And so the very convenient death of the Marshal aroused public opinion to such a degree that it was thought wise to publish the findings of the physicians that there was no trace of poison in his body, and that Ornano had died after an attack of dysentery and fever lasting three to four weeks, despite the most careful attentions of his attendants, the use of all possible remedies and treatment by the best and most skilled doctors of Paris. Louis himself had to send a letter giving details of the Marshal's illness to all high officials in the kingdom. Nevertheless, the doubts persisted.

The Vendômes were never brought to trial. They were simply held in captivity until the Grand Prior died after several years of imprisonment, while the Duc de Vendôme was released after four years of captivity without any hope of the governorship of Brittany or any other office being restored to him.

Anne had been summoned to appear before Louis, the Queen-Mother and Richelieu and was accused by the King of a conspiracy against his life in order that she might marry Gaston. She furiously repudiated the charge, declaring that she would gain nothing by such an event; then she reproached the Queen-Mother for persecuting her and ruining her life with the help of her 'creature', the Cardinal. But Louis was not to be appeased. He issued an order, countersigned by Richelieu, which forbade all nobles not attached to Anne's household to enter her apartments, and forbade Anne to grant any private audience without informing the Queen-Mother or the Cardinal, in advance, of whom she wanted to receive and what was the purpose of the interview.

Only one person remained to be dealt with: Mme de Chevreuse. Richelieu insisted that she was the most guilty of them all: 'She has done more harm than any other person.' But after Chalais had repudiated all his allegations against her there was no proof of any guilt on her part. A Royal Council was held to discuss the possibility of arresting her and putting her on trial, but to bring her before the Parlement or any court of justice for criminal proceedings would not only arouse the fury of the great French houses but also of foreign powers. Through her marriage she was a member of the independent house of Lorraine; she was also a friend of the King of England. So after a long discussion Louis decided finally that, as a first step, she should be banished to a distant place. The Château of Dampierre was too near Paris, and, although she was forbidden to have any communication with Anne, Marie could not be trusted.

The Duc de Chevreuse had promised to be responsible for her good behaviour in future, and so he was commissioned to conduct her to a castle in the distant province of Poitou, where she would have to live under continuous surveillance, a prisoner to all intents and purposes. When the news was brought to her, she exploded in fury. She shouted for all to hear that 'the King was an idiot who allowed this buffoon of a Cardinal to give him orders', that they knew little of her, thinking that she had a mind fit only for amusements and coquetry. She would show them that she was capable of more than that. She would see to it that every Frenchman in England should be treated exactly as she was in France. There was nothing in the world that she would not be prepared to suffer to revenge herself.

However, the Duke was already on his way to Dampierre to expedite her departure; but when he reached the château it was empty. Marie had disappeared in the darkness of the night, in spite of all the observers and spies around her.

Chapter III

No one knew how Marie had managed to escape, what route she had taken after her flight, nor her whereabouts, until after some time news reached Paris from Lorraine that she was there in the capital, Nancy, and had on her arrival been warmly welcomed as a dear relative by the young sovereign of Lorraine, Duke Charles IV. Then reports began to come in of the sensational effect that the fascinating personality of the 26-year-old Duchess had produced there: that the chivalrous Duke, five years her junior, had fallen deeply in love with her; that he regarded her not as a refugee seeking asylum in his territory but as a sovereign guest, who had brought to his duchy all the refinements of life at the French Court as well as her own beauty and charm. In her honour he arranged balls, hunts and jousts in which he excelled, and these festivities were greatly enjoyed by the Court of Lorraine. Engravings of these courtly events were made with dedications to Marie, reflecting the prevailing sentiments:

> 'It is you, Madame, whom France has recognized as the luminary of the perfections, and you have come to receive the same approbation from our eyes, our voices and our hearts. We confess that Lorraine has never beheld such charm, so much more glorious in that it is not foreign. Madame, here is the heaven in which your sun should shine naturally . . .'

Richelieu did not believe for one moment that her intention had merely been to exchange the dangerous atmosphere of the French Court for a more pleasant one. He was expecting trouble from her, and to intimidate the Duke he reinforced the garrisons in the three neighbouring bishoprics of Metz, Toul and Verdun and ordered the rebuilding of the citadel of Verdun. When the bishop, at the Duke's request, stopped the rebuilding work and excommunicated the workmen who continued with the job, Richelieu sent a judge to Verdun who declared the excommunication null and void and sentenced the bishop to pay an exorbitant fine.

But if Richelieu imagined he would intimidate the Duke by such measures and make him yield, he misjudged the character of the young and daring Charles who had visions of performing great deeds of valour. Moreover, the Duke had been told by Marie that it was mainly the indecision and weakness of Gaston and the disunity among the great French nobles which had enabled the Cardinal to break their resistance. Every attempt to compromise with Richelieu was bound to fail, because he hated the old-established order of semi-independent liege-lords with the King merely as their acknowledged leader and not as the absolute ruler. Their welfare and the interests of their particular territories counted for nothing. Everything had to be sacrificed in the service of the unrestricted authority of the King, who in reality was no more than a puppet in the hands of the true dictator, the Cardinal.

Charles himself was the independent ruler of Lorraine, which was nominally part of the territory of the Habsburg Holy Roman Emperor; but for some neighbouring fiefs over which he claimed sovereignty he was obliged to pay homage to the King of France, and if Richelieu considered him lacking in obedience, how secure was his position? It seemed, in fact, as if Richelieu wanted to prove to Charles how justified Marie's warnings had been, because he now ordered one of his officials to investigate the right of Charles to these adjoining lands, whereupon most of the claims were declared invalid and a demand was made for the return of these domains to France.

If the affairs of countries and provinces were to remain under the control of their natural lords and were not to fall under the domination of an official responsible only to a far-removed King whose favour he had somehow won, Richelieu had to be stopped, and the only means of doing this was to form a union of all neighbouring powers to break his rule. There was now a unique opportunity to create such a coalition.

The previous year, when the marriage between the sister of Louis and the King of England was being arranged, Buckingham had come to Paris to conclude an alliance with France against Spain, bearing in mind the fact that the French were already fighting against Spanish troops for some Italian possessions. His efforts had been in vain and Richelieu not only concluded a treaty of neutrality with Spain, but even sent French ships with contraband goods to the Spanish Netherlands. These ships had now been captured by the English, and Buckingham had just declared war on France. The only active force against Richelieu's power in France itself were the Huguenots, and already two years previously Richelieu had written in a memorandum to Louis: ' So long as the Huguenots in France are a state within the state, the King cannot be master within his realm.' The last great King of France, Henri IV, had established the rights of the Huguenots, but now, less than twenty years later, this Cardinal was preparing their death-blow. Their stronghold was La Rochelle, on the Atlantic coast, and as Richelieu had no fleet he made himself Controller-General of Shipping and Trade and started to establish a navy. To forestall him, Buckingham was preparing to land troops at La Rochelle.

It did not take Marie long to win Charles over to the idea of a coalition against Richelieu. Soon Buckingham's envoy, Lord Montagu, Earl of Manchester, whom Marie knew from her sojourn in London, arrived in Lorraine, and a great plan of action was devised: further definite allies were to be the Duke of Savoy, whose plans Richelieu was continuously thwarting, and the Comte de Soissons, who had been freed to seek refuge from Richelieu's persecution in Turin. As soon as Buckingham had disembarked his troops at La Rochelle, Savoy and Soissons would simultaneously invade Dauphiné and Provence, where they could join the Huguenots in the south, who, under Rohan, would rise in revolt in Languedoc. Charles would raise an army of 10,000 foot and 1,500 mounted soldiers and march through Champagne towards Paris, and everywhere he would be certain of a welcome. In addition the Emperor promised him 6,000 men if he needed them. Montagu proceeded to Savoy, Marie made contact with her banished friends, and Charles began to reinforce his French frontiers.

Richelieu, who had spies everywhere, was naturally aware of some conspiracy and pursued his campaign against the nobles with increased vigour. Whomsoever he distrusted was dismissed and thrown into a fortress where he was left to perish. The names of those arrested were often not even announced. As the landing of the English at La Rochelle was expected and there was no French fleet to prevent it, Richelieu hired Dutch ships to keep watch around the harbour of La Rochelle, but he had underestimated the feelings of the Dutch Protestants. In Amsterdam riots broke out, and the Dutch ships were withdrawn. Then, in spite of the protests of the burghers of La Rochelle against the violation of their rights, he reinforced the fortifications of the two islands in front of the harbour and put strong garrisons into the forts.

When in July 1627 the English fleet appeared in sight of La Rochelle the inhabitants did not dare to rise in revolt before the English troops had landed, while Buckingham was afraid to land so long as the fortress islands and their garrisons could cut off his retreat. So he landed on the Isle of Ré and began a siege which dragged on without success, and the delay gave Richelieu time to put an army into the field. As long as the English were not on French soil, the waiting allies on their part could not risk beginning a campaign. To spur them on to action Montagu travelled from one to the other, but his efforts were in vain. In November, after nearly four months of siege, Buckingham was compelled to evacuate the island and sail back to England, promising nevertheless to return with a stronger force. In the meantime Richelieu's spies, who in disguise had followed Montagu everywhere, informed the commander of one of the frontier posts that Montagu was near the French frontier, and the commander penetrated with some troops into Lorraine and seized him on the Duke's territory.

Charles immediately demanded Montagu's release and the punishment of the officer who had violated his territory, but the demand was refused by the Queen-Mother who, during the absence of Louis and Richelieu at the siege of La Rochelle, was at the head of the Government in Paris, and Montagu was brought into the Bastille. His capture caused great alarm among the conspirators and especially frightened Queen Anne, with whom Marie had maintained correspondence and who now trembled at the thought of what the papers found on the captive might contain. Any mention of her would mean complete ruin. Fortunately the papers proved to be purely political documents, instructions from the King of England, Montagu's own memoranda and some of his correspondence, including letters from Marie. These papers simply confirmed what Richelieu had expected to find, namely that 'England, Savoy, Lorraine, the Emperor and the heretics in France were all bound together in pernicious designs against the State'; and he concluded his memorandum to Louis with the words: 'This whole business has been set going by Mme de Chevreuse.'

Three months after Montagu's arrest, Louis left Richelieu with the army besieging La Rochelle and returned to Paris, because in the capital signs were becoming increasingly evident that Gaston, who had always been the favourite son of the Queen-Mother, was behaving as if he were the actual ruler, and now his supporters were gathering around him. At the news of the King's return Montagu asked for an audience. He was an envoy of the King of England, kidnapped on foreign territory and therefore unjustly imprisoned in the Bastille. On the strength of this argument he actually obtained an audience and used all his diplomatic skill to present the whole war as the result of misunderstanding.

He declared that the King of England had the greatest affection for Louis and had only taken up arms because Louis seemed not to reciprocate his feelings and had refused to receive Buckingham, who was to bring proposals for friendship. Savoy and Lorraine had joined England because they were wounded by being held in such low regard. Moreover, peace could easily be restored. But, as he particularly stressed in his diplomatic talk, 'The ill-treatment meted out to Mme de Chevreuse, a princess so beloved in England, for whom King Charles entertains a particular affection, must be reconsidered and she must be allowed to return to France.' Indeed he emphasized the point, indicating that in the peace settlement the attitude taken towards Mme Chevreuse would have to be specified.

Louis was so impressed by the talk that, without giving an immediate answer, he wrote to Richelieu describing the interview; the Cardinal was still directing the siege of the desperately resisting fortress of La Rochelle. Richelieu replied that, although the idea of permitting Mme de Chevreuse to return made him hesitate,

'as it was difficult and beyond hope that this lady, being of such an evil disposition, could ever become innocuous, but it might be that, as with malignant planets which increase their malignity when in a constellation they dislike, and on the contrary soften when they come into a position they find pleasing, she too would perhaps relax her malignity a little if she were delivered from exile.'

In the meantime, however, he recommended the release of

Montagu, who was accordingly set free and conducted to the frontier of Lorraine.

On Marie's advice the Duke of Lorraine went to Paris to express his satisfaction with Montagu's release and to clear up any misunderstandings, and again his first request was for Marie's pardon. Thus the relationship between France and two hostile countries and the establishment of peace depended on the attitude of the French Government towards Mme de Chevreuse.

Finally, Richelieu reached the conclusion that it was dangerous to leave her any longer in Lorraine, where she could go on plotting with all sides, and he convinced Louis that it would really be better to have her in France under careful observation. So it was now only a question of finding a formula to preserve the royal dignity in order to prevent the mention of her name in a clause of the peace treaty. Accordingly it was declared that her pardon was a reward to the Duc de Chevreuse for his loyal and devoted service. The conditions of her return, however, were that she should reside in Dampierre and not come to Paris or any other place where the King or the Queen might be. The Duc de Chevreuse agreed with everything and undertook to make his wife comply with all conditions. He wrote to her but received no reply.

When he wrote this letter the news had just arrived that on August 23, 1628, Buckingham had been murdered just as he was preparing for a new expedition to La Rochelle. The report gave Marie such a shock that she fainted and had to be bled several times before she regained consciousness; even after she had recovered she remained in utter despair. This event destroyed all her hopes. All her efforts had been in vain. Richelieu had won.

Crestfallen she returned to France with her baby daughter, Charlotte-Marie, to whom she had given birth in Lorraine, and discouraged, she retired to the residence assigned to her. In her seclusion at Dampierre she could only observe the course of events from afar.

When La Rochelle surrendered after being ravaged by hunger, its population of 25,000 having been reduced to 5,000, who were barely alive, Richelieu showed that he had waged not a religious war but one merely for political control. The survivors were allowed to practise their religion again, but the city was deprived of all its privileges. The office of Mayor was abolished, the towers were pulled down, the walls razed to the ground, the moats filled in, and a strong garrison was left to quell any signs of resistance.

Having finished with La Rochelle, Richelieu revealed his next intentions. The main power of the Huguenots lay in the south of France, and his plan was to begin with the destruction of their strongholds there. But a question of external politics came up which had to be dealt with first: that of the succession to Mantua.

There were two rivals for the throne: the Duc de Nevers and the Duke of Savoy. The Duke of Savoy had shown himself as Richelieu's opponent, while the Duc de Nevers was merely a nobleman of high rank. A foothold in Italy would place France in a strategic position in case of need to cut the connection between Spain and the Austrian Habsburgs. So Richelieu decided in favour of the Duc de Nevers.

But here he encountered the resistance of the Queen-Mother. The Duke of Savoy was married to her daughter, another sister of Louis, and she saw no reason why he should be denied a means of extending his meagre territories. The Cardinal seemed to have forgotten that whatever position he had now reached, he owed it to her and to her perseverance in overcoming the resistance of Louis to his appointment to the Royal Council. Instead of being grateful and remaining her devoted partisan, he now acted as if his will was supreme. Contrary to her wishes, he managed to win Louis' support for his plan, and they both set off with the army against Savoy, whose insignificant frontier defences were soon overrun; the fortress of Casale was taken and Mantua was thus barred to the Duke.

After this began the campaign against the Huguenots in Langue-doc and Provence. Despite the outstanding bravery of the Huguenots, their strongholds were razed to the ground one after the other, and everywhere there was looting and butchery. Those who escaped hanging were sent to the galleys. Finally the Duc de Rohan, the leader of the Huguenots, had to flee to Venice, and the Peace of Alais stipulated that all Protestant fortifications in the kingdom must be razed, although the freedom of religion, as settled by Henri IV in the Edict of Nantes, was confirmed.

Richelieu had achieved his aim, but when he now set out on his return journey to Paris his mood was not at all a happy one. The King's frame of mind was uncertain. His jealousy had been aroused and his suspicion awakened that this new favourite, too, was forgetting that his position was completely dependent on His Majesty's will and that his successes were won only in pursuance of tasks entrusted to him. Besides, Richelieu's spies, who kept him constantly informed about every intrigue at Court, sent him the disturbing news that the 'Devouts', a new Ultra-Catholic party, were furious that the Cardinal had accorded to the Huguenots the right to exercise their religion freely, and the Queen-Mother, enraged by the loss of her control over her son, had aligned herself with them. If Richelieu, her 'creature', forgot that only her influence and persistence had brought him to the position he now occupied, she had not forgotten it. If he no longer felt the need to respect her opinions and wishes, his 'ingratitude' infuriated her, and if he tried to circumvent her influence upon Louis in order to get him completely under his own control, she would have her revenge. And so she spared no effort in trying to convince Louis that Richelieu should be dismissed.

Faced with this enmity, Richelieu looked for allies at Court and, fully aware of the hostility between the Queen-Mother and Anne, tried to win the young Queen to his side. From his headquarters in the south he had already started to write to her, and although Anne had no more sympathy for him than for her mother-in-law she understood that this sudden friendly approach could be utilized.

She was, of course, secretly corresponding with Marie in Dampierre, but as each letter from the one to the other had to be carried by some particularly trustworthy messenger, this was a cumbersome and unsatisfactory procedure. Anne longed to be reunited with her friend again, and the unexpected attention on the part of the Cardinal offered an opportunity which would at the same time put the honesty of his friendship to the test. So in her reply to his letter she asked him to end the exile of Mme de Chevreuse and to readmit her to Court.

Richelieu not only complied with her wish but wrote himself to Marie, inviting her to return to Court and assuring her of his friendship. Although Marie was naturally informed of the Queen's request, this letter came as a happy surprise, because rumours were circulating that Louis intended to transfer her from Dampierre to the fortress of Vincennes, where she would be completely cut off from the outer world. She did not waste any time, but went immediately to Court, where her readmission was at once understood as a ruse of the Cardinal to win the Queen's support in his fight against the Queen-Mother. Then, when Richelieu himself returned to Paris, Marie naturally went to thank him for his kindness and was received in a very friendly fashion.

They had a long and quite thorough discussion about the existing state of affairs, and both understood that collaboration would be of mutual advantage. Marie assured him of her desire to be of service to the King and to him, and he in return promised her his support and protection. It was an agreement to alter their conduct towards each other and to be friends rather than foes, although neither thought for a moment of abandoning their own ideas or principles. Nevertheless, their new relationship aroused amazement among the courtiers. When Marie wrote letters to the Cardinal containing items of information which could be useful to him, or even visited him, whilst he upheld and protected Marie instead of bitterly criticizing her, the courtiers could think of only one explanation for this remarkable change, and soon there was talk of a love affair between the Cardinal and Mme de Chevreuse.

Meanwhile, the Queen-Mother's attacks continued without interruption. At every Council meeting there were wild scenes, and when Gaston, already furious at not having been given a position of command in the army, was also refused the office of Governor of Burgundy and Champagne, which he wanted, he suddenly left France, declaring that he did not feel safe in his own country. The pent-up hatred of the Queen-Mother against Richelieu broke loose. She declared that if Louis needed this 'yellow-faced, arrogant invalid' for his foreign policy, she would not interfere, but she did not want to have anything to do with him. Richelieu, once again correctly assessing the King's character, offered his resignation, which, as he had expected, was not accepted. Instead Louis managed to arrange a kind of truce by luring Gaston back to France with the offer of a large sum of money and the governorship of Amboise and Orléans, which were some distance away from all the frontiers. Anyway, as the Spanish troops had in the meantime resumed their activity in the Po valley, trying to regain Mantua, Richelieu was appointed by Louis 'Commander-in-Chief of the Army' and had to depart for Italy.

Louis himself wanted to go with the army, but Richelieu had received reports from the front that plague and dysentery had broken out there and he could not risk exposing the King to this danger, for he knew that if Louis should die Gaston would inherit the throne and the Queen-Mother would take over the government. Thus he insisted that Louis should remain in Paris under the pretext of the need for keeping watch on Champagne and any possible moves on the Emperor's part. He had just offered the King of Sweden, Gustavus Adolphus, a yearly subsidy of 600,000 livres for the invasion of Germany, in spite of the fact that the treasury was completely empty and the country's economy in desperate straits.

France herself needed an army of 50,000 men for the planned Italian campaign and to maintain security at home, but only had disorganized and unreliable troops commanded by men whom Richelieu considered untrustworthy. Under these conditions, and with a total lack of preparation, he had to embark on one of his most risky enterprises, from which his enemies expected complete failure. But instead of marching against the Spaniards, he moved his troops once more against Savoy. The unprepared Savoyards fled at the first encounter, and he was able to occupy the Savoyard fortress of Pinerolo, thereby securing the shortest line of communication with France for the supply of provisions which the Duke of Savoy refused to provide. When the Duke of Savoy, who had so far remained neutral, now declared himself an ally of Spain and called for Spanish aid, this was only to be expected. For the moment Richelieu felt safe and started negotiations for an armistice with Spain.

It was therefore not a military problem which at that moment worried the Cardinal, but the daily information he received about the intrigues at Court, and he saw no other way of securing his own position than by writing to Louis informing him that his presence at the battle-front had now become necessary. That call was just what Louis wanted and he immediately set out. But the whole Court followed him as far as Lyons, from which place he managed to continue his journey to Grenoble with only his immediate advisers. Here he was awaited by Richelieu; a Council of War was held and the Cardinal insisted that the attack on Savoy should continue. Louis, still under the influence of the Court's attitude towards Richelieu, and mindful of the growing unrest in the country and the flood of inflammatory pamphlets which were appearing in Paris, asked the Cardinal to go to Lyons and there to explain the situation. But finally he went himself, accompanied by the Cardinal; 6,000 men of this motley army deserted when they witnessed the departure of the King as well as of the Commander-in-Chief.

When after a short visit to Lyons they both returned to Grenoble they heard that the Duke of Savoy was everywhere spreading the news that pestilence in Piedmont and Upper Italy had reduced the French army by a third, that riots were breaking out in France, and that the whole war had been instigated by the Cardinal. Of course, Richelieu could not dare to expose the King to the dangers of the infested area and insisted on his return to Lyons. In Lyons, Louis had again to face pressure from the Court and soon called once more for Richelieu, who arrived to find himself a target from every direction. The war was not going well. The Commander of the Imperial forces had retaken Mantua and the peace negotiations had run into difficulties; and, even when the armistice of Rivalto could finally be signed with Spain, the atmosphere at Court, dominated by the Queen-Mother, did not improve. Then, as the last blow, Louis suddenly became ill with a high fever.

Three days later a violent attack of dysentery developed. Everybody blamed Richelieu for the illness, as it was he who had called the King into the infected area. The Queen-Mother and Anne, who had reached a reconciliation with Louis after he had confessed that he was troubled on account of the estrangement between them, remained day and night at the King's bedside. But after a week his condition deteriorated to such an extent that the twenty-nine-year-old King was thought to be dying. A mass was celebrated in his room and he received the last sacraments.

In the other rooms plans were being made that, immediately after the King's death, Richelieu should be put to death and Gaston, in accordance with the King's will, should assume the crown. As Gaston's wife had died some time earlier, after giving birth to a daughter, he was in a position to marry Anne. Richelieu naturally knew of these plans and it was said that as a precautionary measure he had obtained a promise from the Duc de Montmorency

56

to accompany him with an escort of 500 guards to the safety of the papal enclave at Avignon.

However, Louis did not die; an abscess in his bowel burst, and his condition began to improve. But when two years later Richelieu had one of his special courts condemn the Duc de Montmorency to death for rebellion, it was generally said that he did so because he had shown his fear and weakness to the Duc.

As soon as the King's recovery was certain, the Queen-Mother started to work on him again: she declared that every evil emanated from Richelieu: all the uncertainty at the frontiers, all the hatred within the country, all the discord within the Court, all the dissatisfaction among the nobles – everything was Richelieu's doing. In the end she even managed to get from him a kind of promise to end the Cardinal's dominance; but when in complete misconception of her son's character she continued with her prodding and demanded Richelieu's immediate dismissal, the King became restive and declared that he would make his decision only in Paris. At the same time he warned Richelieu that his mother was displeased with him and urgently recommended him 'to seek a reconciliation'.

When the autumn fogs came in October, and Louis wanted to leave for Paris, he decided that Richelieu should accompany him and that the Queen-Mother with the Court officials should follow a few days later. Shortly after Louis' departure the news arrived in Lyons that at the Congress of Ratisbon a peace treaty and an alliance with the Emperor had been signed by the French envoys, whereupon great rejoicing broke out and festivities were organized. But Richelieu had no intention of abandoning his policy of fomenting resistance in Germany to the Habsburgs. When the agreement reached him in Roanne he tore the document up, declaring that the envoys had exceeded their powers. They were only to concern themselves with the Italian conflict and not to make any treaties with the Emperor which would mean the sacrifice of the interests of France and her allies.

Louis was apprehensive and ordered the Cardinal to remain in Roanne and to explain his action to the Queen-Mother and government officials, while he himself set out alone for Paris. Richelieu's attitude caused great bitterness at Court and despair in the country as the news of his rejection of the peace agreement spread from town to town. The hatred for Richelieu rose and the only hope left was his downfall, now definitely anticipated. In the meantime he played the part of an affectionate host to the Queen-Mother: he arranged a marvellous journey down the Loire, with extravagant entertainments, while troops accompanied the great barges on both sides of the river. The Queen-Mother seemed to be pleased and appeared amiable, but when on arrival in Paris Louis asked Richelieu, 'How did you get on with Her Majesty?' and received the reply that everything had gone off excellently, the King only said, 'You are mistaken!' The hostile mood continued, and when Richelieu asked for an audience with the King to discuss the intrigues, Louis refused to receive him.

It now seemed to be only a question of when and how the Cardinal's dismissal would take place. The Queen-Mother had not the temperament to bide her time and to wait patiently. When her son came to visit her in the Palais du Luxembourg, she ordered all doors leading to her reception room to be locked so that nobody could enter because she wanted to have the King to herself without risk of being disturbed. But she had scarcely begun to describe how impossible the prevailing conditions were, when a seldom-used door leading from the room into a windowless passage to the private chapel suddenly opened and Richelieu entered unannounced with the remark, 'You are certainly speaking about me.' The Queen-Mother, surprised and enraged, exploded in fury. Losing all control of herself she burst into a torrent of accusation and abuse.

Richelieu's attitude was one of complete humility. He sank to his knees and begged the Queen-Mother's pardon if he had in any way unwittingly offended her and assured her of his loyalty and devotion. But it was all in vain; her rage could not be assuaged, and the torrent of abuse against the Cardinal continued, until Louis, embarrassed, put an end to the scene by leaving without a word.

Richelieu believed himself lost, and this opinion was shared by the courtiers who now thronged the Queen-Mother's palace, congratulating her and manoeuvring for some advantageous position in the expected changes in the Government, when it became known that the King had driven straight to his hunting lodge at Versailles while Richelieu, downhearted, was preparing to leave Paris in anticipation of his banishment. But he had taken great care to surround Louis with his protégés, and when the King, now in the solitude of Versailles, lamented to his valet Saint Simon about the difficult decision he had to face, he heard nothing but praise for the humble attitude of the Cardinal before the Queen-Mother. Other attendants similarly commended the Cardinal's submissiveness and virtue, and Louis very soon found himself faced with the prospect, either to dismiss the Cardinal, which meant that he must then continually suffer his mother's moods and, whenever he wanted to act independently, be prepared for scenes like the one he had just experienced, or to retain the Cardinal, humble and devoted as he had shown himself to be, in a situation in which the King's word must be law.

On the occasion of his appointment as First Minister, Richelieu had promised Louis 'to ruin the Huguenots, to debase the pride of the great nobles, to reduce all his subjects to do their duty, and in doing so to raise His, the King's name even among foreign nations to the point which was rightfully due to Him'. The first part of the promise he had already fulfilled; the present disturbances were caused by the arrogance of those who were unwilling to discharge their main duty, which was to serve the will of the King obediently, thus preventing the elevation of his name to the honour due to him among foreign nations. Should he dismiss such a man simply because his enemies had won the ear of the Queen-Mother?

During the evening of the same day Richelieu received the summons to come to Versailles and was given a benevolent and gracious reception. Louis assured him of his undiminished favour and the security of his position.

This day, November 10, 1630, when the hopes of the Queen-Mother and her adherents were frustrated, is remembered in history as the 'Day of Dupes', and from the very next day Richelieu showed that he was not going to be satisfied with the King's favour alone, but that he was resolved to establish an iron rule over all branches of the Government and of the military command. One by one all the adherents of the Queen-Mother, all the supporters of her views were dismissed, banished from Court, discharged from their commanding posts in the army and often brought to trial under trumped-up charges. Dubious of the reaction of the judges, Richelieu put every one of them before a Special Tribunal. He dismissed Marillac, the Chancellor and Keeper of the Great Seal, replaced him by Châteauneuf, who had previously been French Ambassador to England, and put him at the head of this Court. And at every opportunity Châteauneuf contrived to get from the Special Tribunal the desired sentence: death. The arrests continued ceaselessly, the castles of the arrested were razed to the ground, their possessions were confiscated and the money, although it was so badly needed for the war, was often spent recklessly, partly for the building of Richelieu's luxurious palaces. He himself confessed that he did not know anything about financial matters.

The only man against whom he could not take proceedings was Gaston, the heir to the throne, and Gaston withdrew from Court and moved to Orléans, where he was Regent and where he started to gather the discontented nobles around him. In order to prevent the possibility of a conspiracy between his mother and his brother, Louis moved with the Queen-Mother, Anne and the whole Court to Compiègne, where he could keep everybody under the strictest supervision, and tried to bring about a reconciliation between his mother and Richelieu. But his efforts failed completely. At first they led to a new outburst on her part, then to lamentations and to an attitude of deep sorrow. Finally she refused to see the Cardinal at all and ceased to attend the Council meetings over which he presided.

Richelieu took advantage of her absence at the very next meeting of the Ministerial Council, now composed entirely of his own confidants, to clarify the situation. At first he did not convey what he had in mind, and only when commanded by Louis to speak openly and without restraint did he declare that:

'the Emperor, the Kings of Spain and of England, and the Dukes of Savoy and Lorraine were jealous of the glory of the King and were seeking to create trouble in his kingdom by secret intrigues and subversion. The malcontents enjoyed the approval of the Queen and in particular the support of the Queen-Mother, who was dangerous because to her was attributed the power to achieve the dismissal of the King's Minister. In the midst of such intrigues and insubordination it was impossible to maintain order. Therefore there were only two solutions feasible: either his own resignation or the assignment to the Queen-Mother of some place of residence where she would be cut off from the possibility of any communication with the rebels. But that was a decision which only the King alone could make.'

Louis, seeing himself confronted with the alternative of either dismissing the man whom he had just assured of his confidence and of the safety of his position, or of detaining his own mother, at first faltered. But finally he gave the order that the Court should proceed to Paris without the Queen-Mother. The departure took place at night in such secrecy that Anne was awakened after it was dark with the order to follow the King at once without first approaching the Queen-Mother, who was told next morning that the Court had left and that she was to be escorted to Moulins, where she would be entrusted with the government of the province.

Her bitter retort was, 'The mother of the King and subordinate to the man who rules his mind,' and she wrote to Louis that his action 'would find neither the approval of God nor of men'. She refused to leave and was forced to watch her physician and her ladies arrested and removed in spite of her protests. However, she herself continued to stay at Compiègne, as it would not have been possible to use force against the Queen-Mother. Richelieu had to be satisfied with keeping her under strict observation, surrounded by troops and prevented from communicating with the outside world.

But Gaston was still in Orléans, trying to make it the centre of resistance. He published an open letter, charging Richelieu with ruling the country for his own vainglory, seizing and executing people at his pleasure and committing one arbitrary act after the other. He alleged that the prisons were filled with the King's most devoted friends and that the whole country was groaning under the tyranny of this insolent priest. He accused him of not ending the Italian war, because thereby he would remain indispensable, and of ruining the country by continually raising taxes and reducing the people to such poverty that they were dying miserably of hunger. Louis had gone forward with a strong force against Gaston, who fled at the approach of the King, but his open letter continued to circulate and various riots had to be suppressed; these circumstances were again skilfully exploited by Richelieu.

Various parts of the country had their special provincial privileges, which gave expression to the particular customs and traditions of the population. Some had independent assemblies, provincial Parlements which, like the Parlement of Paris, were not political bodies of people's representatives but high courts of justice with extensive powers. These regional authorities imposed certain limitations on the power of the distant King over the region. Richelieu was therefore determined to abolish them, and if a rising in any of these provinces took place and was put down, the Cardinal saw to it that the region received the King's pardon only after renouncing these ancient privileges, thus strengthening the King's authority.

After Gaston's flight Louis issued a proclamation declaring his brother, together with his supporters, guilty of high treason, but the Paris Parlement refused to accept this decree and the King had to dismiss various councillors and magistrates and to tell the Parlement that, although it had the right to present its views, it had not the right to interfere in State affairs, and forced it to register his decree. Yet more and more anti-Richelieu pamphlets were beginning to appear and all public sympathy turned to the Queen-Mother, who had now been held as a captive of the State at Compiègne for four months.

Richelieu recognized that the King was becoming increasingly unpopular because of the treatment of his mother, and conceived a new plan: he reduced the guards and relaxed the watch on her movements, and Marie de Medici fell into his trap. Remembering her flight from Blois twelve years ago, she hoped to repeat her escape, but as she now had no Duc d'Epernon waiting for her with his troops, she selected among her attendants a young relative of the Governor of La Capelle, which was situated near Flanders, and asked for his assistance. One evening a coach was waiting for her when she took a walk in the Forest of Compiègne and she was taken quickly to La Capelle. But Richelieu's instructions travelled faster still; she found all the town gates closed to her and after a few days of searching desperately for a safe refuge she could see no other way to safety than by crossing the frontier to Flanders.

That was precisely what Richelieu had wanted: Marie de Medici had joined the country's enemies. Now Louis ordered all her possessions in France to be confiscated and forbade any correspondence with her. The mother of the King of France, of the Queen of England and of the Queen of Spain had to live in poverty as an exile, on a pittance which Philip IV of Spain agreed to pay her out of charity.

Chapter IV

To the astonishment of the Court, Mme de Chevreuse had kept quietly aloof during the whole of the campaign against the Queen-Mother and even after her downfall. Was it that she could see no point in exchanging the dominance of the Cardinal for the rule of some favourite of the Queen-Mother, whose only aim would be to satisfy her royal ambitions, or had she really become the Cardinal's friend? Richelieu himself believed the latter. When she became suspicious that he had disclosed some secret information which she had entrusted to him, he wrote to her to allay her suspicions in such humble terms as would scarcely have been expected from a man in his position:

'I would have shown myself completely unworthy of the honour of your friendship if I were able to misuse it in this way. If I had committed such a cowardly act as to disclose to others what you graciously entrusted to me, I would moreover have betrayed myself. I must confess I had not imagined that you could think me capable of such a crime. But instead of getting irritated, I only plead with you to trust me more in future and to believe that I would prefer to act against my principles rather than miss any opportunity to prove to you on any occasion that I am prepared to make greater sacrifices than these for your sake.'

He very soon had an opportunity to convey to her what an exceptional position she held. The Duc de Chevreuse had quarrelled with another high nobleman who had lampooned him, and catching sight of this noble in a courtyard of the Louvre, Chevreuse drew his sword and launched an attack. They had scarcely exchanged a few strokes when the guards intervened and separated them; duelling was a severely punishable offence and Chevreuse, as the aggressor, jumped on his horse and fled. Richelieu proved his friendship to Marie by telling her that her husband need not be afraid and could come back, restricting him to Dampierre for two weeks only.

4. Cardinal Richelieu, from a portrait by Ph. de Champaigne (National Gallery, London)

Henry Rich, Earl of Holland, from an
engraving by Wilhelm Pass

5. George Villiers, Duke of Buckingham, after
a painting by Vandyck

Marie on her part rendered the Cardinal what he considered to be an important service: as Charles of Lorraine was raising an army, Marie travelled to see him and induced him to pretend that he was doing so only because he owed allegiance to the Emperor and wanted to be ready in case his services were required somewhere in Germany. Later she even persuaded him to come to France and to make a treaty, but her real reason for undertaking this task was her anxiety for the safety and the quasi-independence of her friend's duchy which, now isolated, was at the mercy of the French. However, Richelieu took her action as evidence of her goodwill; and afterwards, when on his flight from Orléans Gaston went to Lorraine, Richelieu dictated letters for her to write to Charles and she complied again, assuring the Cardinal, 'I am resolved to prove to you through all my actions that I remain, as my duty demands, always your devoted and obedient servant'. But this time her real motive was to protect the interests of Anne, as Gaston wanted to marry the younger sister of Charles. Incidentally, on this occasion Charles did not obey; the marriage took place in absolute secrecy, and was in fact kept secret for a long time. When Gaston, after collecting a band of mercenaries in Brussels, returned through Lorraine and invaded France, Charles joined his brother-in-law and had, after Gaston's repulse, to suffer the loss of some of his territories.

But now Marie's thoughts were concentrated on Anne, from whom she was once more inseparable. Her friend's reconciliation with Louis had not survived long after the King's illness. Shortly after the return to Paris she was again confined to her rooms and felt herself so surrounded by spies that she did not 'feel safe even in her bedchamber'. These were naturally Richelieu's spies; but what were the intentions of the Cardinal and of the King concerning her that made it necessary that she should be kept under such strict surveillance?

With the complete disruption of the royal family, Richelieu's tenure of power was secured and he could turn his attention to fulfilling the second part of his promise to the King to 'curb the pride of the high nobles' by crushing those who still nurtured some feeling of independence and whose hold on points of vantage in the country could make them dangerous. So for them a new wave of persecution, detention and exile commenced, accompanied by the confiscation of their possessions. But behind the political reasons there was also the Cardinal's desire for complete and undisputed dominance over Louis, and although Anne was again out of favour, her position as Queen could make her dangerous. Thus Marie felt it to be of the utmost importance to discover in advance his designs in relation to Anne, and the only way was by winning over some close collaborator of the Cardinal with all the necessary information. Marie's choice was no less a person than the Marquis de Châteauneuf.

To induce the Marquis de Châteauneuf, the man whom Richelieu had made the Keeper of the Great Seal, in charge of the Special Tribunals to obtain the required death sentence in every case, to work against the Cardinal seemed an impossible and crazy plan. But for Marie the idea meant a special personal triumph, because it was Châteauneuf who, as French Ambassador in England, had earlier described her as ill-disposed and had maligned her at the time when Charles I had interceded on her behalf. His support had to be won.

Thus the 51-year-old Marquis suddenly found himself the object of the attention of the most beautiful ladies of Anne's Court, who all craved to be in his company and to enjoy the pleasure of his conversation, until finally Mme de Chevreuse herself, now thirty-two years-old, appeared on the scene with all her charm and wit, just as eager to see him. He very soon surrendered completely.

Marie played out a love affair with him, raising his self-esteem and at the same time awakening his jealousy against the Cardinal, who, she pretended, was trying to impose his unwanted affections upon her. She strictly refrained from any interference in, or even mention of Châteauneuf's official activity. When his Tribunal pronounced the death sentence against the Duc de Montmorency, Marshal of France and Governor of Languedoc, who had tried to help Gaston with his mercenaries 'to free the King from the Cardinal's yoke', the sentence aroused horror among the highest nobility, and a torrent of pleas for mercy and of abuse against Châteauneuf broke out; but she did not join in either, because she knew that all the pleas would be in vain and that Châteauneuf had simply done what Richelieu demanded from him.

What she was aiming for was to awaken in Châteauneuf the feeling that he himself might be as good a man, if not a better one to fill the position now held by the Cardinal, and that he would perform the functions of this office with greater justice and more clemency. Once the idea had been implanted in his mind, she proceeded to convince him that she even knew how he could reach this position. Her own feelings concerning the Queen-Mother were well known, but in the present circumstances Marie de Medici could be used to attain the desired goal. She had been expelled because she had refused to let herself be dominated by her former favourite. That was an injustice in the eyes of the whole of Europe. If the English Court could be persuaded to give her temporary asylum and then demand from the King that she be allowed to return to France, Louis would be forced to sacrifice the Cardinal rather than risk a new rupture with England under the prevailing conditions. And once Richelieu was dismissed, who else was there but Châteauneuf to fill his position and re-establish peace and prosperity in the country.

The best method to bring about this desired change was to approach the Chevalier de Jars, a banished noble who had been received in England not as an exile but as an honoured guest, playing tennis with the King and visiting the Queen. He was in a position to persuade King Charles to act accordingly and would be willing to do so. Thus contact was made with de Jars, letters went to and fro, while Louis with the whole Court, as was now his custom because he distrusted everybody and did not want to leave anybody unwatched in Paris, moved to Toulouse to see that nothing prevented the sentence of death passed on Montmorency from being carried out. While the Court was waiting in Toulouse, the idea arose to make a detour to La Rochelle afterwards to show to the whole Court the glorious deeds of the army which had led to the conquest of the impregnable Huguenot fortress. But after the execution of Montmorency had taken place Louis appeared to feel a need for solitude and went to Fontainebleau, leaving Richelieu to take the Court to La Rochelle.

On the way, in Bordeaux, Richelieu suddenly fell ill. The fever rose so alarmingly that after a few days he was thought to be dying. The hope of deliverance from his rule made the mood of the Court gayer and gayer; balls and festivities were being held every day. But instead of dying Richelieu started to recover slowly and one day, while he was still on his sick-bed, his spies brought to him a letter from Châteauneuf to Mme de Chevreuse which they had intercepted and in which his trusted Keeper of the Great Seal gloated over his illness.

Marie had repeatedly warned Châteauneuf to beware of the Cardinal, 'for he is spying on us, both you and me', and was always extremely anxious to meet her friend 'without the Cardinal's knowledge'. Now this letter could not fail to awaken Richelieu's suspicion. Nevertheless, he continued to keep his feelings, both about the joyfulness of the Court and the attitude of his closest collaborator, strictly under control and waited silently until after nearly two months of illness he was sufficiently restored to be carried in a litter to Paris.

On the way, near Etampes, he was joined by Louis, who came to meet him, but as Châteauneuf was always present, Richelieu could only show the letter to the King during a short secret consultation. Richelieu must still have believed in Marie's good intentions but the King's animosity against her was undiminished, as the letter which he wrote to the Cardinal about a week later shows:

'I have just received the news that a craftsman, newly arrived from England, has gone to wait on Mme de Chevreuse at Jouarre. If she herself reports it to you, this could be regarded as a sign of her amendment; if she says nothing of it, confess at least, for the last time, that she is deceiving you and is laughing at both of us, you as well as me.'

And he shows the reason for his hatred and the feelings which activated him by continuing:

'I will confess to you that two things vex me beyond measure and sometimes rob me of my sleep – the insolence of Parlement and the mockery of people whom you think you know, but who scoff at me and also at you. You know how I trust you in every undertaking that concerns me; believe what I tell you about these two matters, and we shall set them right.'

So it had been in vain that, as soon as Richelieu started on his way back to Paris, Marie had admonished Châteauneuf: 'I want you to appear to be displeased with me and to despise me. I know this will be painful to you, but nevertheless you must obey me in this. It is absolutely necessary. Beware of the Cardinal.' The

68

warning came too late: the French Ambassador in London had arranged a burglary at the home of the Chevalier de Jars and had then sent the stolen papers to Richelieu. Now he had in his hands a full revelation of the plot to induce the King and the Queen of England to bring about the return of the Queen-Mother to France, which would mean his being superseded by Châteauneuf. But in the stolen papers there was no mention of Mme de Chevreuse. Only when Châteauneuf was arrested and his house was searched did the whole correspondence between her and the Keeper of the Great Seal fall into the Cardinal's hands, some fifty letters in all which had been decoded for him.

Now he could read her sneers at him, her contempt for the feelings which, as she assured her lover, he had for her. She declared that she despised the favour of the Cardinal; she did not fear his power; she detested his person and had as much contempt for him as she had affection for Châteauneuf.

'I take no more account of the Cardinal's favour than of his power, and I shall never do anything unworthy of myself, either because of the benefits that I might derive from the one, or because of the harm that I might suffer from the other. Believe this if you wish to do me justice. . . .'

'I believe that I am destined to become the object of the folly of madmen. The Cardinal certainly proves it to me. . . .'

'. . . the Cardinal's tyranny increases every moment. He storms and raves because I do not go to see him. Twice I have written to him compliments of which he is unworthy – a thing I should never have done but for the way in which I was pestered by my husband, who told me that this was the only way to buy peace. I believe that the King's favour has raised the Cardinal's presumption to a pitch which cannot be surpassed. He imagines that he will frighten me by his anger, and is persuaded, in my opinion, that there is nothing I will not do to appease him. But I prefer to perish rather than submit to the Cardinal. His pride is intolerable to me. . . .'

'I believe the Cardinal wishes no longer to leave me in peace day or night; even at nine o'clock in the morning he sends somebody to enquire how I am doing . . . Although I am unwell,

I am unwilling to stop without telling you how my visit to the Cardinal passed off. He spoke to me of his passion, which he said had reached such a point as to be the cause of his illness, owing to his vexation at my behaviour towards him. He complained at great length of my conduct, particularly in regard to M. de Châteauneuf, and concluded by declaring that he had no desire to live any longer tormented by the sentiments that he cherished for Mme de Chevreuse, unless she showed that those she entertained for him were different from what they had been in the past. To which Mme de Chevreuse replied that she had always endeavoured to give the Cardinal reason to be satisfied with her, and that she wished to do so more than ever. . . .'

Later she informs Châteauneuf:

'. . . the Cardinal is better disposed towards me than he has been since his return. He wrote to me this evening that he is extremely distressed by my illness; that all the favours of the King gave him no pleasure in the condition in which I am, and that the gaiety which M. de Châteauneuf had shown today had caused him to alter his opinion that he loves Mme de Chevreuse, and that if Mme de Chevreuse had witnessed his demeanour, she would judge him to be either the most dissembling or the least affectionate man in the world, and that she would be obliged never to love or to trust you anymore. . . .'

Describing an incidental meeting with Richelieu in Anne's apartments, she shows that she had in no way lost her sharp wit and uses her tongue without restraint:

'He paid the Queen in my presence the most incredible compliments and gave her the highest praise, while to me he showed a deliberate coldness, disdain and neglect. At some teasing remark to me on his part, I ridiculed him in such a manner, without paying the slightest attention to his lofty position, that he was more astonished than indignant, changing his attitude at once and showing the greatest politeness and humility when speaking to me. I do not know whether he did this in order not to reveal his bad humour in the presence of the Queen or whether he was afraid to spoil his relationship with me. Tomorrow at two o'clock I shall see him and tell you afterwards what happened. I assure you that only death can tear me away from you.'

Another time she writes:

'The Cardinal's pride is intolerable to me. He recently said to my husband that my humour was unbearable to a sensitive person like himself, and that he had resolved to show no special attention to me in future, as I did not deserve either his friendship or his confidence. ... The Cardinal's mad vagaries are wonderful! He sent for me and made strange complaints that I was perpetually sparring with him in the presence of Lord Jermyn, in order that the said Lord might return to his country and recount how little respect I have for him.'

Whatever these letters meant, whether the stories were true or just invented to awaken the jealousy of her friend, these written proofs of the way in which he had been tricked by a woman and betrayed by a man whom he had trusted must have enraged the Cardinal. Nevertheless, he could not risk them becoming publicly known. Besides, among the other correspondence found at the search there were letters from the Queen of England, the King's sister, from Lord Holland and from some favourites of Gaston which would implicate the heir to the throne whom Richelieu was trying to induce to return to France. Thus Châteauneuf could not be brought before a Court for trial, and when questioned about the conspiracy his answer was, 'Just women's nonsense and silly talk.' So he was simply confined to the citadel of Angoulême.

Richelieu's mood is reflected in his memoirs when he writes:

'Châteauneuf was involved in all the Court cabals; and particularly in the intrigues of our factious ladies, the principal of whom was the Duchesse de Chevreuse, whose conduct and noxious spirit have often displeased the King as she has never failed to join the plots raised against his crown; more than this, she has always appeared as a dangerous leader of factions.'

Nevertheless he must have been impressed by Marie's personality and perhaps still hoped to win her eventually to his cause as he had done with many of his other opponents, because the only action he took against her was to banish her once more to Dampierre.

However, such a mild punishment did not satisfy the antagonism of Louis to Mme de Chevreuse. Besides, Dampierre was too near to Paris, and although Marie was forbidden to have any communication with Anne, she could easily send some trusted servant with letters to the Queen and receive her replies – in fact she went so far as to take the risk travelling to the capital, disguised as a peasant woman, in order to see Anne when she was passing a night in the convent of Val-de-Grâce, afterwards returning to Dampierre before daybreak. Even though he knew nothing of such escapades, Louis ordered that Mme de Chevreuse should be banished to some distant isolated place, far away from Paris and from any frontier. It is strange to note that the Cardinal, before putting this order into effect and despite Marie's opinion of him, expressed in her letters to Châteauneuf, asked the King for permission to visit her. But a woman like Mme de Chevreuse, scorning danger and ignorant of fear and weakness, passionately – almost heroically – pursuing her course would, in a sense, have his admiration. To the Cardinal she may have been a gallant soldier in the wrong pay.

The reply which Louis gave him was typical:

'You ask me whether you may go once more to see Mme de Chevreuse. You know very well that the visit will not be agreeable to me. This having been said, do what you will and be assured that I shall always be to you the best sovereign that the world has ever seen.'

After such a reply and the particular underlining by the King that he was the sovereign, there could no longer be any question of seeing Mme de Chevreuse. Thus a coach, escorted by a guard of musketeers, drove into the courtyard of Dampierre and the officer in command showed Marie the order bidding him to escort her to the Château de Milly which had belonged to Luynes and was now to become her place of exile. The château was isolated, some miles from Tours but also not too far from Couzières, where Marie had spent her childhood. So she knew everybody of importance in the region.

It was the Archbishop of Tours who had conducted her marriage ceremony with Luynes, and she lost no time in winning the now octogenarian churchman over completely. She had recently begun legal proceedings against her husband, who was recklessly squandering the riches which Luynes had left to her.

She was endeavouring to obtain a legal separation of property and soon had the Lieutenant-General of Tours representing her financial interests before Parlement, which, as the highest court in the country, had to give judgment on the matter. She was also able to get a house in Tours as a town-residence, and it was not long before she resumed her relations with the outside world.

Nevertheless, it was a solitary life for her, with rare breaks in the monotony, such as visits from Marsillac, the son of La Rochefoucauld, who on his journeys from Paris to his château at Verteuil always stopped to see her and, as a devoted adherent of the Queen, brought her letters from Anne and carried back her replies. Then came Lord Montagu, who had been sent by the King of England on a diplomatic mission to France; he visited Anne and naturally did not miss the opportunity of going to Tours and seeing Mme de Chevreuse. He introduced to her the young Count Craft, who also succumbed to her charms and was very soon ecstatically in love with her, as his letters, which were intercepted, show:

He wrote to her from Calais:

'I cannot stay at any place for two days without sending you a message. I hope, when I have finished this letter, to be able to embark for England, and the thought of you will sustain me in all difficulties. How often do I look at your picture and kiss it! I beg you also to think sometimes of me and of the great love which I carry for you in my heart, now and forever. I belong to you with body and soul for all eternity!'

And after his arrival in London he wrote her:

'You are the only one whom I love with all my heart and all my soul for all my life! ... My soul can only gain some comfort from the thought that there is nothing in the whole world worthy to be compared with you!'

Making such an impact on the hearts of men, she found no difficulty in selecting among the increasing number of visitors the most reliable and trustworthy ones as messengers for conveying coded letters not only to and from Anne but anywhere she wanted. With the help of the English Ambassador she established communication with the Queen of England and her English friends. When, after another campaign against Lorraine, Charles had to leave his duchy and go to Brussels, she found means of communicating with him. She was informed of all that happened at the Court and in the country as well as of all events in the international sphere.

Conditions in France had steadily worsened. To get the money for paying the allies who fought against the Emperor in Germany, taxes were continually increased and the methods employed to collect them served to enrich the tax-collectors whilst robbing the poor of their last means of supporting themselves. Thousands of them died as debtors in prisons, and uprisings in various regions were suppressed with every conceivable cruelty. But Richelieu did not believe in allowing the people tolerable living conditions. As he wrote in his *Political Testament*: 'All politicians agree that when the people are too comfortable it is impossible to keep them within the bounds of their duty. . . . They must be compared to mules which, being used to burdens, are spoilt more by rest than by labour.' Now his foreign policy was imposing on the country an ever-increasing burden of armaments, particularly since France herself had entered the war after the victory of the Imperial and Spanish troops over the Swedes at Nördlingen. But although his purpose was to reduce the power of the Habsburgs over the German states his declaration of war was issued not against the Emperor but merely against Spain.

The war against Spain made Anne's position still more difficult. As a Spanish princess she was now regarded with even greater suspicion and spied upon to make sure that she was not supplying any information to the enemy. The Archduchess Infanta Isabel had died in Brussels and Anne's favourite brother, the Cardinal Infante Don Ferdinand, became Governor of the Low Countries. Was it possible that she was in secret correspondence with him?

Four years previously, at the time of the departure from Compiègne, the King had assigned a new lady-in-waiting to her, namely the eighteen-year-old Marie de Hautefort, who had previously been attached to the Court of the Queen-Mother and in whom he seemed to take an affectionate interest. Anne's initial dislike of the girl soon changed into a devoted friendship when she realized the great affection the new lady-in-waiting had for her and also the fact that Louis' interest in the beautiful and clever girl was purely platonic. He simply enjoyed her lively conversation; she gave him the feeling of solace and personal attachment which he sought, so that he could confide to her his innermost thoughts and feelings and be certain of her discretion. Richelieu's immediate efforts to obtain her services were promptly rejected by her and she missed no opportunity of arousing the King's annoyance over the Cardinal's dominance, and also of reproaching him on the subject of his treatment of Anne. Her endeavour to reconcile Louis with the Queen, however, only led to quarrels with him and he warned her: 'Mark my words – you love and support an ungrateful woman. Wait and see how one day she will repay you for your services.'

Nevertheless, when Richelieu tried to set him against Mlle de Hautefort, Louis resentfully rejected any comments about his feelings towards her and Richelieu waited patiently until a new quarrel occurred between the two of them. Then he advised the King to punish the girl for her unshakable devotion to Anne by pretending to transfer the honour of his attentions to another beautiful lady-in-waiting, Louise-Angélique de la Fayette. The ruse succeeded only too well. Mlle de la Fayette was an accomplished singer, and when at the next Court entertainment she was induced to sing some verses which Louis himself had written and set to music, the King fell in love with her.

He found in Louise de la Fayette a still more soothing and discreet companion who kept completely silent about everything he confided to her, took an interest in all his pastimes and pleasures and was conveniently not attached to Anne. Again Richelieu failed in his efforts to win her, and she managed to confirm in the King his dislike of further interference on the part of the Cardinal by instilling in him the feeling that by giving in so much to Richelieu he was failing to maintain the dignity of the crown. He began to listen to every observation that she made, drew his own conclusions and then behaved so obstinately in some matters of secondary importance that Richelieu became uneasy.

The war had also taken a bad turn. The French armies everywhere suffered reverses. Spain menaced Languedoc and Provence; troops from the Low Countries invaded Champagne; Charles of Lorraine was victorious in the east; and when the enemy marched into Picardy, took the town of Corbie and forced the passage of the Somme, thus opening the road to Paris, the mood of the people became so threatening that Richelieu did not dare to show himself in public. An army under the Comte de Soissons was the last defence of the capital, and when the enemy tried to turn its flank, Richelieu, in his search for a scapegoat who could be declared responsible for the successes of the enemy, turned upon Anne.

Was she not a Spaniard? Had she not tauntingly advised Mlle de la Fayette to exhort the King to make a swift peace with Spain as long as he could hope for advantageous terms? Was she perhaps still in clandestine correspondence with her brothers, informing them of the weak points in French armaments? ... Now he felt afraid for the security of his own position, and in order to demonstrate his devotion and to retain the King's affection he made a will leaving to Louis his magnificent Hôtel de Richelieu with all contents – which he had recently built, notwithstanding the increasing poverty in the country – thus restoring his riches to his royal benefactor instead of bequeathing them to his relatives.

His calculation proved to be correct. Louis was very pleased with the display of such devotion, and as at the same time the hesitation on the part of the Spanish commanders saved Paris and the French recaptured Corbie, the Cardinal regained his confidence. Gaston, who with Soissons was now in command of the army in Picardy, recognized that there was no other way to get rid of Richelieu than by assassination. He devised a plan, but at the last moment, when he was due to give his officers the signal to fall upon the Cardinal who was alone with him, his courage failed and Richelieu departed unharmed. When some time later Louis, after giving his brother a particularly friendly reception, recommended that he should now go to Paris, Gaston, remembering many similar occasions in the past when the King's pronounced friendliness had been a prelude to calamity, fled instead to Auvergne, which was under his rule; and Soissons, who had also taken part in the plot, escaped to the independent fortress of Sedan, belonging to the Duc de Bouillon.

Now, there were only two persons left close to the crown who were openly opposed to the Cardinal's dominance over the King: Anne and Louise de la Fayette. The King's assiduously nourished distrust of Anne, who lived under constant observation, surrounded by Richelieu's spies, made Mlle de la Fayette appear to be the more dangerous of the two, particularly as Louis' feelings for her had become so affectionate that he one day offered her an establishment at Versailles and the title of duchess. Although she declined the offer, the idea of an omnipotent mistress spurred Richelieu to immediate action. She had in her youth been destined to become a nun, and now the Cardinal induced her confessor to insist that her soul was in danger if she gave up her true vocation and did not renounce the world. The same instruction was also given to the King's confessor: Did he want to be the cause of the damnation of the soul of the girl he loved?

In spite of Louis' bitter sorrow and the girl's deep misgivings, in the end the insistent pressure of the ecclesiastics prevailed. Louis had to declare 'that man has no right to oppose the will of God', and Louise de la Fayette entered the Convent of the Visitation. The only solace that remained to the King was, whenever he happened to be in Paris, to go to the convent and to talk to her through the grille about his worries and anxieties.

At the time Richelieu's spies brought to him not only a letter from Anne to Mme de Chevreuse, with whom she was forbidden to correspond, but also reports that when Anne retired to the convent of Val-de-Grâce, her periodical 'place of retreat', to 'meditate', there were letters waiting for her there and the man who brought them came again to fetch her replies. This messenger was Anne's devoted 'cloak-bearer' La Porte, now restored to his former post as her 'valet de chambre', and he was followed as he went to the English Embassy, from where he returned to the convent, leaving a letter there at the grille. Finally the Cardinal's spies managed to intercept a letter from Anne to the Spanish Ambassador in Brussels, the Marquis de Mirabel. Although in it she only complained that she had not received a reply from her brother, the Cardinal Infante, that was sufficient.

Richelieu communicated the news to Louis, and at the next meeting of the State Council he made a speech, declaring that to his belief Anne 'had made important political disclosures, the proofs of which must exist in the convent of Val-de-Grâce' and accused her of treasonable relations and illicit correspondence not only with Mme de Chevreuse but also with Spanish ministers in London and Brussels, with Marie de Medici and the Queen of England. Louis, in his antipathy to Anne, was also in favour of taking the strongest possible measures against her; but that was too much for the other members of the Council. They were aghast.

Even the Chancellor Séguier, a devoted adherent of Richelieu, declared that 'an arrest of the Queen and her arraignment on a charge of high treason would damage the prestige of the monarchy and be prejudicial to the dignity of the crown'. He recommended instead to exact from her a full confession and to take measures to prevent the possibility of any future offence. All the councillors agreed to his advice, and so he was commanded by the King to proceed with his inquisitions, and the Archbishop of Paris was ordered to accompany the Chancellor to Val-de-Grâce.

Anne, completely ignorant of the decisions taken, had to follow Louis to Chantilly, and immediately on her departure La Porte was arrested and imprisoned in the Bastille. Two letters to Mme de Chevreuse were found on him, one containing just harmless gossip, the other warning Marie that her idea to visit the Queen at the Louvre to confer on important matters was 'too perilous'. He also carried a letter from Marie to himself, asking him to get the Queen interested in a quick settlement of the law-suit between her and the Duc de Chevreuse. That gave the Cardinal the idea that, as Marie seemed to be in money difficulties, he could perhaps win her over by sending her a considerable sum of money as proof of his good intentions, and to ask her incidentally whether she had exchanged letters with Anne and whether she had planned to risk coming to Paris to see her friend.

Marie immediately understood that her letters had been intercepted and, as no news from Anne arrived, that some dangerous development was taking place. She answered that she would accept the Cardinal's money with thanks, not as a gift but only as a provisional loan; she confessed that she had corresponded with the Queen and indeed wanted to come to Paris in disguise, but only in order to influence the Queen to seek a better understanding with the Cardinal. Did this not mean that, in order to serve him, she was prepared to undertake the risk of being arrested and imprisoned?

The search of the convent of Val-de-Grâce was equally unsuccessful. The Chancellor reported that the abbess must have received some warning in advance and had destroyed all papers with the exception of a few trivial letters. She maintained that she had not the slightest knowledge of what the Queen did when she retired to her cell during her stay in the convent and what the letters arriving for her contained. But although nothing incriminating was found, the abbess was relieved of her post and transferred to another convent as an ordinary nun. La Porte, in spite of all threats, again refused to give any information without a direct order from the Queen to whom he owed allegiance. Thus the only way to get any incriminating evidence was to extract a confession from Anne herself. But when the Chancellor arrived and showed her the intercepted letter to the Marquis de Mirabel, she tried to snatch it from him, and there was a wild scene.

After a few days, when she found out how much of her activity was known, she asked in a mood of complete despair for Richelieu to come and see her. In the condition in which she was, trembling in fear, it did not take him long, after he had promised to obtain for her the King's pardon, to get her to admit that she had written to her brothers, the King of Spain and the Cardinal Infante in Brussels, but that the letters were only about their well-being and did not contain anything harmful to the interests of France or of the King; yes, she had complained about the way she was being treated; yes, she had warned them that rumours were going round about a reconciliation with the Duke of Lorraine and an alliance with England; yes, she had received from Mirabel the advice to be careful. In making these admissions she humiliated herself before the Cardinal, promising that she would feel an everlasting obligation towards him if he would only extricate her from her present plight.

Richelieu was satisfied with his victory over his last opponent at Court and the confession he had obtained from her, but when he reported to the King, Louis demanded to have this confession in the Queen's own handwriting, in which she must admit all her wrongdoings, beg for forgiveness and promise never again to commit such offences. This confession was dictated to Anne word by word, ending with the assurance of complete repentance and obedience; and when Richelieu brought this humiliating paper to the King, he agreed to pardon the Queen, but showed his continuing distrust by ordering her not to write any letters at all except in the presence of one of her ladies-in-waiting, who was Richelieu's spy and who would communicate their contents to the King.

This new prohibition was for Anne a shattering blow. She

understood that the enquiry was continuing, the interrogation of La Porte in the Bastille was still proceeding, and he had to be informed of her own confession and what she had said in order that their testimonies coincided. Secondly, Marie had to be advised of all the events, because if the Cardinal and the King were so afraid of any communication with foreign countries, Mme de Chevreuse in Tours was bound to be their target. Already rumours were circulating that she intended to flee from France to England and that Richelieu had warned the King that to let her out of the country would be too great a risk, as she had

'such a dangerous mind that once abroad she would create unforeseeable complications. She is in the most intimate connection with the Duke of Lorraine and with the English Court. If she leaves France she will prevent the Duke of Lorraine from coming to any understanding with us, on her own behalf and that of the Queen who is on the side of the Spaniards. She would again create difficulties in England and lead the English according to her will and always find a cause for new trouble. I think it is therefore better not to let her out of the country.'

In this desperate situation Anne appealed to Mlle de Hautefort for help, and Marie de Hautefort acted at once. The Chevalier de Jars had long ago been lured away from London back to France and had later been confined in the Bastille, where he still remained as a prisoner at large, which meant that he was permitted to receive relatives as visitors. So Mlle de Hautefort, dressed as a servant-maid in a large coarse cloak, with a wide hood concealing her face, went into the Bastille, and pretending to be the wife of his valet who had fallen ill, gained access to him and succeeded in persuading him to pass on a letter from Anne to La Porte. The second task was still more difficult to fulfil, but Mlle de Hautefort managed to carry it out by sending a cousin of hers to Tours. He arrived just in time before two interrogators from the Cardinal came upon the scene with a letter from Richelieu in which he wrote:

'I have asked M. du Dorat to see you about a matter which will certainly be of importance also to you. As I always feel prompted to give to you fresh proofs of my affection and my readiness to

6. Marie de Rohan, Madame de Chevreuse, from a portrait by Daret

7. Ciaude de Lorraine, Duc de Chevreuse, from an engraving by
Balthaser Moncornet

be of service to you, I beg you to be completely open with me and you can feel sure that if you act accordingly, you will emerge from this affair without the slightest discomfort, as you have done before in no less difficult situations.'

Thus Marie was prepared for their questioning. They assured her of the Cardinal's goodwill; that she did not need to have any apprehension and should openly disclose to them all her connections with people abroad. She reciprocated by insisting on her feelings of friendship for the Cardinal but regretted to have to disappoint them by confessing that she now no longer had any connection with Charles of Lorraine, the Queen of England or anybody else of interest to the Cardinal. All efforts to obtain any confession from her were in vain. But then she realized that if the interrogators could get no satisfactory information from her, they had been ordered to arrest her. Meanwhile, while she was in church, a little prayer-book bound in red was slipped to her. That was a signal of immediate danger prearranged with Anne, in case no other method of warning was possible.

Now Marie did not waste a single moment. She rushed to her friend, the octogenarian Archbishop of Tours, a native of Béarn, declaring that her life was in danger and that she had to flee to a place close to the frontier. He gave her the description of the best route to Béarn and even a letter of recommendation to one of his nephews there. To Richelieu's envoys she declared herself ill and exhausted and in need of an evening drive by herself in her coach, which in the past had always restored her. When darkness fell she stopped the coach at a prearranged place in the forest and emerged from it dressed as a man in a black coat, jerkin and breeches with high boots. Her face was daubed with a mixture of soot and brick-dust, and on her head she wore a fair wig fastened with a black silk bandage tied around her forehead, as if she had a wound. Two trusted servants were waiting there with a saddled third horse. The coach was sent back on a circuitous route to Tours and ordered to stop in front of her mansion with all the usual ceremony as if she were to descend, in case spies were about. The house-servants had been instructed not to let in any visitors, using the pretext that she was ill. Then she mounted the horse held ready for her and the three riders galloped away in a southerly direction. In

F

this manner Mme de Chevreuse left the place of her remote exile after four long years.

The riders carried neither linen nor change of clothes, neither bags nor parcels. In her pockets Marie had only the remainder of the money that Richelieu had sent to her. They rode throughout the night and the whole of the next day, then they slept in a hostelry on the wayside and next morning were again in the saddle. By evening they reached Ruffec, where Marie slept a couple of hours, then ate, and, although scarcely able to hold herself in the saddle, rode again through the night until they were approaching the Château de Verteuil, which belonged to the Duc de la Roche-foucauld, where his son Marsillac lived.

He was still in bed when a letter was brought to him:

'Monsieur, I am a French nobleman and implore your help to save my liberty and perhaps my life. I had to fight a duel and have killed a nobleman of high rank; I am being pursued and that forces me to flee from France in order to escape arrest. I hope you will be generous enough to help me, even if you do not know my name. I need a carriage and a valet and riding horses for my men.'

Tradition demanded that he comply with the request, since Richelieu had forbidden duelling and some duellists had in fact been executed. He sent a carriage with one of his trusted servants, and now the 37-year-old Mme de Chevreuse could exchange the saddle for a cushioned seat and sleep while she journeyed. When they reached another place, also belonging to La Rochefoucauld, the man in charge of it, Potet, who had previously been in the service of Luynes, recognized Marie in spite of her disguise and declared himself happy to be at her disposal. When she now wanted to consult the papers in which the Archbishop had described the route she should follow to the frontier, these could not be found. They must have been lost, but Potet, also a Basque, knew the right route and she let herself be led by him. Next day she sent back her own two servants, as she assumed that by now the hunt for her would already have started and they could be recognized. She also let Marsillac's coach return and bought herself a horse.

With Potet and Marsillac's servant she crossed the River Garonne at Agen, and afraid to approach the usual coaching-inns they slept wherever they could find shelter. One of the hostelries was so dirty that Marie preferred to sleep on straw in a barn, where a peasant woman discovered her, saying, 'This is the prettiest boy I have ever seen in my life,' and brought her four fresh eggs. When the three reached the little town of Cahuzac her attendants went to the attorney Malbâti, and informed him that they were accompanying a friend of Marsillac. Marie explained to him that she wanted to take the waters at Bagnères because of 'a wound received in a recent duel which causes me a lot of pain'.

Malbâti had planned to go to a place of pilgrimage in the south later on, but she persuaded him to accompany her now, and also sent Marsillac's servant home. After they had started out, Malbâti began to feel suspicious about the young man and questioned Potet, but got nothing from him; so the next day he asked his mysterious companion who he might be. Marie answered that she was the Duc d'Enghien, the son of the Prince de Condé, but refused any further information with the excuse that duelling was forbidden and now carried the death penalty, and to stress the noble tradition of the duel she started reciting verses from Corneille's *Le Cid*, which had just recently been performed at Court.

When after four days they reached Bagnères she enquired from the innkeeper whether the waters there or perhaps at another near-by resort were more beneficial and when told that this depended on the nature of the illness, she said that she knew a physician at Tarbes whom she would consult. Then she went to the spring and there saw a gentleman from Paris who recognized her. She made him swear to keep her presence a secret and asked him whether he could provide her with a guide to Spain. Fortunately he knew one, and everything was arranged.

The following day, when Malbâti hesitated about accompanying her to Tarbes, she told him that she was not d'Enghien and if he consented to come with her she would tell him who she really was. Once they had started out she led him deeper into the Pyrénées instead of to Tarbes, and when they reached the little hut where she was to meet the guide, she told Malbâti that she was Mme de Chevreuse and was leaving France against her will, but that she would rather 'throw herself into the fire then be shut up in a prison'. She considered herself blameless and was crossing into Spain as the only means of escape from France, but would in a few days be on her way to England.

Malbâti tried to warn her of the dangers of the mountains, of robbers lying in wait, but she replied that she knew of a hospice a few leagues from the frontier where there were Spanish priests who would give her asylum, and from there she would write to the Viceroy of Saragossa asking him to send her a coach. When the guide, a Spanish peasant, arrived, the moment of parting had come. She threw her arms around Malbâti's neck and kissed him. Then she took her horse by the bridle and, ten days after she had left Tours, walked up the mountain path and safely reached the hospice where she was received by the monks with great kindness.

Marie had been very wise in trying to avoid the usual highways and the commonly frequented inns in fear of pursuit. At Tours she had left a letter for the Lieutenant-General saying that she was leaving France and asking him to look after her interests as previously. When the letter was handed to him, he immediately informed the Duc de Chevreuse, who was at once interviewed by an agent of Richelieu. Then the Lieutenant-General wrote another letter to his own brother, who was a councillor and member of the Parlement of Paris, which had just recently given judgment in favour of Marie's petition for the 'separation of property'.

Richelieu's first action was to send an investigator to Tours, and when the direction of Marie's flight was discovered couriers were despatched in pursuit and all authorities in the districts through which she was expected to travel were ordered to stop her. But they could find no trace of the fugitive. It took two weeks to establish the precise route which she had taken, and by that time she was already across the frontier.

The excitement which her flight had caused, and the orders given to the pursuing emissaries to convince her that no action against her had been intended and that her flight was a mistake, made the prosecution of the persons involved impossible. Only Marsillac, about whom rumours were circulating that he had learned that the young man was in reality Mme de Chevreuse – and as anyway the loan of a coach to a duellist was a punishable offence – was kept for a week in the Bastille and then released.

Chapter V

After a few days' rest in the hospice, Marie descended the Pyrénées on the Spanish side and rode to St Esteban, the nearest stronghold, from where she informed the Viceroy of Saragossa of her presence; at the same time she sent a letter to Richelieu saying that, on receipt of a warning that she was to be arrested for things 'of which she had never even thought', she was forced to assume that her destruction had been decided upon. Since the Châteauneuf affair she had avoided everything that could warrant any suspicion, but now she had heard that the accusers pretended to have in their hands proof of her offences. That was the reason why she had left France.

The Viceroy of Saragossa immediately informed Madrid of the arrival of Mme de Chevreuse on Spanish soil and sent her a coach. From Madrid came the order that the Duchess was to be received with every mark of distinction. From France came the message: 'We do not write to Spain.'

Thus she proceeded from Saragossa to Madrid. *En route* she was met by a royal coach drawn by six horses and escorted by officers of the Court, in which she continued her journey. On her arrival in the capital she was acclaimed by the crowd. She received magnificent presents and was installed in the state apartments of the palace. The grandees and the courtiers vied with one another in doing her homage; and she was soon as fêted and as popular as she had been in England and Lorraine and was overwhelmed with all kinds of attention. The King offered her a permanent place at his Court and a pension, but she refused to accept any Spanish money. She had many friendly talks with the Queen, Elisabeth of France, who was eager to hear everything about the life at the French Court which she had left as a little girl. The powerful Prime Minister, Olivarez, very soon recognized that this beautiful woman not only possessed great charm and intelligence, but also had an excellent grasp and knowledge of politics and affairs of state, and he liked to discuss them with her and hear her opinion.

The reception accorded to her and the audience granted by the 32-year-old King Philip IV were immediately used by the gossip-mongers in Paris, implying that Philip had fallen in love with Marie. Louis himself did not miss the opportunity to declare to Anne in front of the whole Court that the King of Spain had slept with Mme de Chevreuse.

However, with the war between France and Spain still in progress, Marie could not continue to remain as an honoured guest in enemy country and decided to proceed to neutral England. King Charles immediately granted her permission to take up residence in London, and the King of Spain ordered one of the Court officials to accompany her to Fuenterrabia, where a ship-of-war from England was already waiting for her. When she disembarked at Portsmouth, Montagu and other Court nobles were there to welcome her, and the reception in London was even more cordial than in Madrid. She met all the friends she had made thirteen years before, and they all remembered her previous sojourn with delight. Henriette-Marie regarded her as an old friend; Charles I assigned to her a lodging in the garden of Whitehall and, despite the alarming financial position of the government, offered to provide her with a pension suitable to her rank, which she, however, declined to accept although she foresaw difficulties in finding means to defray her living expenses. She had finally obtained from the Parlement in Paris the decree for 'the separation of property between her and her husband', but now she received the information that the French Government, after her flight, had refused to let the decree take effect and had sequestrated all her estates. Charles and Henriette-Marie wrote to Louis and Queen Anne, as well as to Richelieu, on behalf of Mme de Chevreuse, but all their efforts were in vain, and so Marie saw herself forced to buy on credit everything she needed.

Nevertheless, neither her adventures nor her present difficult situation seemed to have diminished her verve or depressed her; as Lord Holland wrote to a friend who had fled to Italy from the dismal atmosphere of the Court, embattled with Parliament: 'She makes our life as gay as yours is in Turin.'

It was shortly before Marie's arrival in England that all the courts in Europe had been surprised by the public announcement of the French government that the Queen of France was expecting a child. Anne's sudden pregnancy, after nearly twenty-three years of marriage, while the alienation between the royal couple had never been so complete, naturally provided a topic of conversation everywhere. The Queen resided in the Louvre, the King seldom set foot in that palace except for State audiences and receptions, and spent his time wandering between Fontainebleau and Chantilly. His apartments in the Louvre actually stood empty without being furnished, and this very circumstance served to explain Anne's pregnancy. In the previous December Louis had proceeded from Versailles to his hunting lodge at St Maur and while passing through Paris decided to visit Mlle de la Fayette in her convent in order to have a long talk with her. During this time a terrible storm broke out, followed by torrential rain, so that he could neither travel to St Maur nor return to Versailles, and finally the Captain of the Guard had persuaded him to go to the Louvre to dine with Anne and to spend the night there.

This explanation was naturally treated everywhere as just an official cover spread by Anne's entourage as soon as she became pregnant, and to satisfy the King. Lampoons, pamphlets, satires full of speculation as to who the real father of the expected child might be were printed and circulated in all countries. Everybody understood that giving birth to an heir was of prime necessity for Anne. The King's health was steadily deteriorating, his nerves were shaken by intermittent attacks of fever, and he could die at any time. Then the crown would go to Gaston, now married again, and that would mean the end of Anne as Queen, while an heir would make her Queen-Regent. Some of the pamphleteers went so far as to ascribe the fatherhood to Richelieu, because, under Gaston, Marie de Medici would return and that could cost him his life, while a Dauphin would make him all-powerful during the long period of minority. And the satirists bewailed the calamities which would befall Europe with a son of Richelieu wearing the crown.

These pamphlets naturally penetrated into Court circles and sharpened the distrust which Louis felt. His attitude to Anne had not changed in the least; he made a point of ignoring her ostensibly, did not visit her in her retreat in St Germain and seemed to show no interest in the expected event. However, the news of the pregnancy gave Marie, who had not been in touch with Anne since her flight, the opportunity to write a letter of congratulations to the Queen from London, and the arrival of this letter aroused in government circles the hope of getting Mme de Chevreuse back into their power. It was too dangerous to let her stay abroad. As Richelieu had foreseen, the French émigrés were already clustering around her in London. She could influence all the opponents of France at foreign courts; she could join Marie de Medici's clique.

In her letter of congratulations she wrote of her deep sorrow that she had been forced to leave France and the Queen in order 'not to expose herself to the evil consequences of the unjustified accusations against her'. Only bitter necessity had driven her to flee to Spain, where 'the deep esteem felt for the Queen had secured her a better reception and better treatment than she deserved'. Now in England, a land maintaining friendly relations with France, she hoped that her letters from this country would not give the Queen cause for any dissatisfaction, and she finished her letter of congratulations by pleading for Anne's help: 'May the protection of Your Majesty shelter me from the evils which the anger of the King and the bad graces of the Cardinal can inflict on me.'

Knowing full well that the letter would be perused by Richelieu or even by the King himself, she added that she did not dare to speak to His Majesty of her ill-fortune and the sufferings which unjust suspicions had brought upon her, nor could she do so to Richelieu, but felt assured that the Queen, by her generosity, would do it on her behalf, thus 'rendering agreeable what might be importunate if it came from me'.

The letter also contained a confidential note, begging Anne, who had once borrowed a large sum from her while she was Superintendent of the Queen's household, to refund to Richelieu the money which he had sent to Mme de Chevreuse at Tours and which Marie had accepted as a loan. And she concluded her note: 'I have charged the bearer of this to acquaint you with a matter which I cannot forget nor conceal from you. The position in which I find myself deprives me of the means of paying this debt! I beseech you to do so, and moreover, to make known your resentment,' adding that she could never repay the Queen for the benefit which she would thereby bestow on her.

Her official letter of congratulation had the desired effect. After its arrival, Richelieu at first drafted an answer which was to be sent by Anne, containing some humorous remarks about Marie's flight disguised as a man, a reminder not to undertake anything in the country where she was staying which would cause dissatisfaction in France, and giving her the assurance 'that nobody here had any intention of doing her harm'. But after some consideration the idea of such a letter from the Queen was dropped as being too simple to catch Mme de Chevreuse, and instead, Richelieu let her know that her congratulations had been received with thanks and her letter to the Queen had not caused any annoyance, so she could continue to write. She answered him immediately, and a long diplomatic tug-of-war developed with the Cardinal.

Richelieu was no less anxious than Marie to come to an understanding. He feared that she would take advantage of her residence in London to join Marie de Medici's party, which was causing him embarrassment. He was particularly anxious for a rapprochement with Charles IV of Lorraine which would leave him free to concentrate all forces against Austria and Spain, but he knew that there was little chance of effecting this so long as Mme de Chevreuse continued to influence the Duke against him. She had to be persuaded to return.

The Cardinal promised her a royal pardon for everything that she might have committed 'of which His Majesty had cause to complain' so long as she made a complete confession. She replied that she had nothing to confess, since none of her activities had been adverse to her duty to the King. As she was without any means of subsistence and did not want to live at the expense of the King of England, she petitioned for a royal declaration authorizing her to return to France with the guarantee that no action against her would be undertaken. Finally, at the end of February 1639, Richelieu wrote: 'As you feel yourself only guilty of flight from your country, the King has ordered me to inform you that he willingly pardons you for it and for anything else that weighs upon your heart.' The royal declaration which he sent her stated that Louis 'remitted, forgave, pardoned and abolished' all offences committed by her and that she would never be pursued or punished for any of them, and then went on to enumerate these wrongs: 'her flight from Tours without the King's consent, her leaving the country without his permission, her entry into an enemy country and her negotiations with the Duke of Lorraine against the interests of His Majesty'.

Infuriated by the tone of the document and particularly by the last accusation, which she had categorically refuted, she refused to accept it. She wrote to Richelieu's representative:

'After all the assurances given to me, it is now being maintained that I have prevented the Duke of Lorraine from concluding a peace with France and induced him to remain on the side of the Spaniards, an action which I have never contemplated. I can therefore not believe in my security in France nor put any trust in the Cardinal's protection as long as His Eminence will not consent to dispose of these charges by giving me the opportunity to clear myself of this suspicion and so provide me with the necessary assurance of a full pardon of my flight from the country.'

While this correspondence was going on Anne had given birth to a boy, but the King's behaviour at the arrival of the Dauphin showed that his deep dislike of Anne had in no way diminished. When the new-born baby was placed in his arms, he remained cool and detached and had to be prompted to approach the Queen's bed and to embrace her, as etiquette demanded. Then he ordered that the child should be baptized at once and receive the name of Louis. Next day, when the festivities in Paris and the provinces began, he held a council at which the letters to the potentates of Europe and the municipal authorities, announcing the arrival of an heir to throne, were drafted, and then, as soon as he could, he left St Germain for the pleasures of the hunt at Chantilly.

As even the birth of a Dauphin had done nothing to improve the relations between the royal couple, and the King's attitude to the newly-born gave rise to the suspicion that Louis himself did not consider the boy to be his legitimate son, Gaston's supporters advised him to declare the child illegitimate and to take up arms; but Gaston did not dare to take the risk. The only man of prominence absent from St Germain at the birth of the Dauphin was Richelieu, who had remained in St Quentin to follow the campaign in Picardy, and his absence from such an important event mystified the Court. Rumours were circulating that the King had told him that the expected child was in all probability not his, whereupon

Richelieu had answered that any child would be better than none, because it would prevent Gaston from inheriting the crown. The scandalous pamphlets which continued to appear now no longer made an impression on the people. The existence of a Dauphin removed the danger of a civil war in the event of Louis' death, which had already worried the country.

The birth of the Dauphin was welcomed by all, but the fact that there was now a direct heir to the throne also meant the continuation of Richelieu's dictatorship, and Marie in London decided to put into practice her plan to make use of the Queen-Mother. The temperament of Marie de Medici was notorious and the King of England had no wish to have her at his Court, but under Marie's influence Henriette-Marie wrote to her mother inviting her for a visit. Thus Marie de Medici appeared in London, and around her and Mme de Chevreuse a powerful clique of conspirators began to congregate and to work against Richelieu. They managed to induce the King of England to write to Louis, asking him to allow his mother to return to France. But all in vain; Louis remained adamant.

Then Marie declared that she would go to Flanders to negotiate directly with the Spaniards, and Richelieu decided that it was too dangerous to leave this woman abroad. She had to be brought back to France and he sent two emissaries to deal with her under the pretence that he was doing so at the incessant request of the Duc de Chevreuse, and that he himself retained his former feelings of friendship for her. Marie replied:

'I could have had no stronger proof of my husband's affection than his efforts for my return to France, nor could I hold out any hope for their success, if your assistance had not led to such a propitious beginning, that thanks to your friendship I can also hope for a favourable conclusion.'

The emissaries, however, recognized very soon that all their efforts would be wasted without some real concession to Mme de Chevreuse, and Richelieu sent to London a new act of grace from the King which contained no mention of her connection with Charles of Lorraine. In order to make the necessary impression on her this had to be a strictly formal document. At the same time it had to make clear that she was being granted an exceptional act of grace from the King, a complete amnesty, and so she received the following declaration:

'*Louis, by the grace of God, King of France and Navarre to all present and to come, Greeting:*

'We have no greater displeasure than when we see ourselves obliged, by the necessity of the welfare and repose of our State, to allow the course of justice to proceed to some example of severity, in order to maintain our subjects in their duty and those of the highest rank in the obedience that they owe to us. And, on the contrary, it is a great satisfaction to us when, by the acknowledgment of their faults, they give us cause to forgive them. Our cousin, the Duchesse de Chevreuse, has as much knowledge as any one in the world that our inclination is to clemency rather than to rigour; whereof, being now wishful to bestow upon her a peculiar proof, in the matter of her last departure from the realm, contrary to the order and the express command that she had from us to remain in our town of Tours, and her sojourn in an enemy's country, and *other faults* that she may have committed in consequence against the fidelity and service that she owes to us, we make known that we have favourably received her very humble petition, on the subject of the said faults, and by these presents, signed by our own hand, we have remitted, quitted, pardoned, and annulled, do remit, quit, pardon and annul for our cousin, the Duchesse de Chevreuse, the fault that she has committed in leaving our town of Tours against the express command that we had given her to remain there, together with her departure from our realm without our permission and her withdrawal into the country of our declared enemies, and generally all other crimes and faults that she may have committed in consequence against our intentions and the service and fidelity that she owes us. It is our pleasure that, for the said faults, she may not be able henceforth to be called to account in any fashion whatsoever, and, in respect of this, we impose perpetual silence on our Attorney-General and their substitutes present and to come, and have restored and do restore her to the same station in which she was previous to them. Therefore, we give command to our trusty and well-beloved Counsellors, the persons holding our Court of Parlement at Paris, to register our present grace and pardon, and suffer and allow our said cousin, the Duchesse de Chevreuse, fully and peacefully to enjoy her property, and to ratify it without requiring our said cousin to appear before them, from which we have dispensed and do dispense her by our special grace, full power, and royal authority. For such is our pleasure. And so that this matter may be firm and stable for all time, we have caused our seal to be placed upon the said propositions, saving in all else our right and authority.

'Given at Saint-Germain-en-Laie, in the month of March, in the year of Grace 1639, and in the twenty-ninth of our reign.
(Signed) *Louis, par le Roy – Bouthillier*."

Despite the wide terms of this declaration, Marie's caution was not entirely disarmed. Did this special mention of 'all crimes and faults that she might have committed' not indicate that she remained under suspicion of other activities to which she had not confessed and which might still be investigated once she was back in France? Still, this document no longer made any mention of the Duke of Lorraine and Marie felt that she could risk the return.

As she had told Richelieu's emissaries that she wished to go to Dampierre, the Cardinal finally replied that the King had accorded her permission to reside at Dampierre, on condition that she would not visit Paris 'either secretly or openly'. That meant that she would be kept there under even stricter supervision than at Tours, without the right of ever appearing at Anne's court. This restriction upset Marie. She demanded permission to return with full freedom to live wherever she wanted. Richelieu replied that before her flight she had been obliged to stay in Touraine, and she had done nothing in the meantime that would justify granting her liberty of movement. The emissaries managed to convince her that permission to return to Dampierre was just a first step, and that if she recognized her previous mistakes and behaved in an appropriate manner the right of free movement would follow, while Marie on her part promised not to maintain any connection, at home or abroad, with any person disliked or mistrusted by the King. So it seemed that all difficulties were overcome and that she would now go back to France, when suddenly the emissaries and the Cardinal received a letter from her expressing her feelings of gratitude but also her deep regret that she was prevented from returning. Immediate enquiry revealed the cause: de Mme Chevreuse's creditors had declared that they would not let her leave before her debts of about 12,000 livres had been paid.

Richelieu sent 18,000 livres and the preparations for her journey home could thus proceed. She bade farewell to all her friends, wrote to King Charles, who already engaged in the civil war, was with his army in Newcastle, thanking him for all his kindness and for having given her shelter. The Queen arranged for a ship to sail in about two weeks from Dover to Dieppe, fifteen months after Marie's landing in England, while in Dieppe the Duc de Chevreuse was to arrange for a coach and two horses to be waiting for her, when she unexpectedly received an anonymous letter warning her not to return to France as her destruction there had been definitely decided upon. They only wanted to entice her to Dampierre in order to get her into their power. This letter was immediately followed by another from the Duke of Lorraine, who wrote:

'I have received definite evidence of the plot which the Cardinal de Richelieu has devised against you. He wants to lure you back to France with every imaginable promise in order to make you perish miserably. The Marquis de Ville, who has heard him speak with his confidant, de Chavigny, will give you further information on the matter. I am expecting him at any moment, and if I believed that I had sufficient influence upon your mind to hold you back from this decision, I should throw myself at your feet to implore, in the name of everything you cherish, not to hurl yourself towards your certain destruction and to avoid a disaster which would be cruel for the whole world, but more unbearable for me than for any other man on earth!'

This letter, written on May 26, 1639, made Marie send for Boispille, one of Richelieu's envoys, who found her, as he wrote to the Cardinal, 'in extreme distress and unimaginable apprehension'. Though he assured her of her safety, she reminded him that the Cardinal had not given her any security regarding her freedom and her life. The envoys wrote to Richelieu suggesting that in his answer to them he should include his guarantee for her safety, which they would show to her in order to remove present as well as future difficulties. But Richelieu answered only: 'Mme de

94

Chevreuse is worrying completely unnecessarily; she has nothing to fear in France, and if somebody is trying to influence her to the contrary he is deceiving her in the vilest manner.' However, Marie now had the feeling that a trap had been prepared for her and she decided to wait for the Marquis de Ville, a nobleman from Lorraine who had been taken prisoner by the French and put into the Bastille, from where he had recently been released. Owing to illness he was not able to come to London for nearly two months, but when he arrived he confirmed that he had been informed by a man who had overheard a conversation between the Cardinal and his Secretary of State, de Chavigny, in which the Cardinal had declared that he had evidence that Mme de Chevreuse had advised the Duke of Lorraine to refuse a reconciliation with France, and that once they had her back in the country they would force her to confess.

This time Richelieu considered it necessary to reassure her himself, saying, though in a letter couched in very cool terms, that the King found it strange that in spite of his Act of Pardon, which she had received, she was still creating difficulties; but as she seemed to continue to fear punishment about the affair with Lorraine he did not hesitate to declare to her that she would receive a full pardon, and the question of her connection with the Duke of Lorraine would never be raised. Nevertheless her answer was: 'The terrible fright into which I have been put has assailed my mind and my head in such a way that I am not able to return to France immediately,' and she begged him to pardon her weakness. But what had in reality convinced her that she could not risk returning was some information about a conversation between her husband and Anne.

The Queen was supposed to have asked the Duke whether he had any news from his wife. At this time the Duke was extremely anxious for Marie to return, not only because, until the separation of property had become effective, he was in serious financial difficulties, but even more because of the worries his daughters were giving him. Marie had left them in a convent under the Abbess of Jouarre, her sister-in-law, but the Abbess had died the previous year and they were now in his care. He had let them come to a convent near the capital, accompanied by some of the nuns from Jouarre. However, the Archbishop of Paris did not want them there and so had had to take all four girls, aged from eight to twenty-one, together with the accompanying nuns, to Dampierre and was desperately searching for a place for them. Thus, when Anne enquired about Marie, he answered in an aggrieved tone that the Queen knew his wife's circumstances better than he did, since it was she who was preventing her from returning. Anne seemed surprised, and finally replied that she loved his wife dearly and that she very much desired to see her again, but that she could not advise her ever to return.

That warning confirmed Marie's worst fears. There was no possibility of a compromise with this particular government and she resumed her contact with all the circles of émigrés as well as her correspondence with Brussels and Madrid and with the malcontents in France, and day after day despatches reached Richelieu that Mme de Chevreuse was making her house the meeting place for all his enemies and maintaining links with the representatives of foreign powers hostile to the French government. The Marquis de Ville came again to London to recruit a thousand men to fight on the Continent against Richelieu's troops, and she lodged him in her house and used her re-established credit on his behalf. When a new Spanish Ambassador arrived in London, he immediately went to see her, and she gave a great reception to introduce him. She corresponded with the Prince of Savoy, who commanded the Spanish armies fighting in Flanders against the troops of Louis, and she even made contact with the Papal Nuncio, since Rome was now also against Richelieu because of his increasing involvement in the religious war in Germany against the interests of the Catholics. Soon the very mention of her name was sufficient to make Richelieu furious.

It was at this time, now about two years after her arrival in England, that the Duc de Chevreuse, having repeatedly urged Marie to return as she was exposing him and her family to 'terrible difficulties and starvation', received the following reply:

'I ardently desire to see myself again in France in a position to retrieve our fortunes and live quietly with you and my children, but I see so much danger in going there, as I understand affairs, that I cannot risk it, knowing that I cannot work to your advantage or to theirs if I am in trouble. I must therefore patiently seek some safe road which will finally lead me home with the tranquillity of mind which I cannot now find.'

Thus the Duc de Chevreuse applied to Richelieu for permission to go himself to England to bring his wife back, if necessary by force. Although Richelieu did not believe in the success of the mission he gladly gave him permission, the required money and return passports for himself and his wife. However, Marie received the news of the plan and sent him a courier with the message that the instant he arrived in England she would leave the country and flee 'into the domains of the King of Spain'. His answer – that he only wanted to come to see her and discuss with her the situation into which her activity had put him and her children and that the journey could not be postponed – did nothing to allay her fears. Two days before he was due to set out from Paris, she left London, and, accompanied by the Spanish Ambassador, Montagu and other friends, travelled to Rochester from where she embarked for Dunkirk, at that time a port in Spanish Flanders.

When the Duc de Chevreuse heard of her departure he rushed to Richelieu with all the correspondence which had passed between him and his wife, because he was afraid of being accused of conspiracy. Richelieu advised him to write to the King of England, asking him not to grant his wife asylum in his country in future; but the King's reply to the Duc was: 'As your wife is a person of such high standing and has during her presence at my Court not given me the slightest cause for dissatisfaction, I do not see how I could refuse her a permission to return, if she decides to make such a request.'

While the Duc de Chevreuse and Richelieu were defeated at every turn, Marie discovered very soon after her landing in Dunkirk that she had put herself in a desperate situation. She was without money and in Dunkirk had no friends who could help her. She found herself cut off from her international contacts because she knew no trustworthy messengers to carry her letters and bring back the replies. She felt defeated and described her position thus: 'I am ruined and as it were in a desert; nobody gives me the slightest comfort. I cannot see anyone without rendering him an object of suspicion, and my solitude is filled with a thousand mortifications.'

G

In her despair she decided to take the risk of returning to France. To reconnoitre her position she wrote humbly to Louis himself, pleading that ill-fortune was the real source of all her troubles. She had gone to Dunkirk with as much regret as she had previously gone to Spain and with the same determination to leave it as soon as the necessity which had brought her there would permit. She assured him of her deepest respect and affection and of her wish to serve him. Louis did not reply.

She wrote to Anne, appealing to her kind nature and begging her to intercede with the King on her behalf. The letter was intercepted and taken to Louis, who ordered it to be forwarded to the Queen. But Anne was cautious. She refused to accept the letter and returned it unopened, declaring that 'she did not care to open any letter from a person who was behaving like Mme de Chevreuse and who was in a hostile country. She did not know what guile or trickery had made that woman write to her.' Now, as the mother of the Dauphin and secure in the future as Queen-Regent, the first alterations in Anne's character were becoming apparent.

Finally, Marie wrote to Richelieu pleading for his mercy and assuring him that she had left England only out of fright at what her husband would do to her when he came to London. She had always wanted to return to France and besought 'the good grace of the King' and the goodwill of the Cardinal. But the Cardinal did not answer, either.

If Mme de Chevreuse's plight was so desperate, she could safely remain where she was, and the question of Anne's previous offences no longer interested him, for the Queen's whole attitude had changed. She not only made peace with Richelieu, whom she now received with distinct signs of favour, but acted with such submissiveness that she did not even protest when Louis, on Richelieu's instigation, ordered the dismissal of several of her ladies and their replacement by some of the Cardinal's followers. Besides, she was pregnant again and eventually gave birth to a second son.

Now there remained only one more obstacle to Richelieu's complete domination over the King, namely Mlle de Hautefort who, after Mlle de la Fayette's entry into a convent, had again become the centre of the King's attention, in spite of the fact that she was now even more outspoken and that their quarrels became fiercer and lasted longer. None of the Queen's ladies had been able to replace her in the King's favour, and so Richelieu had a new idea: one of his pages-of-honour was a particularly brilliant and handsome youth, Henri Cinq-Mars, whom he instructed carefully and then placed among the King's gentlemen-in-waiting. His calculation proved correct. Louis was soon infatuated with the attractive eighteen-year-old, who was so eagerly participating in all his recreational pleasures and proving himself a good horseman, a skilful snarer of magpies and was even able to give good advice on the management of kennels. It was not long before he became the King's constant companion. As Chancellor Chavigny noted 'Never has the King had a more intense passion for any man than for him. I hear that he said to Mlle de Hautefort that he could no longer pretend to have any affection for her because he had given it all to Cinq-Mars.' When Louis quarrelled once again with Mlle de Hautefort, because of some of her sarcastic remarks about Cinq-Mars, Richelieu acted. He proposed that she should be exiled from Court, for just two weeks, 'to prove to the said lady that she was not the most powerful person in the realm': this would make her more careful in future, and the proposal received the King's consent. He sent her an order to leave the Court next morning without a farewell audience with the King. When she rushed furiously to Anne, all she got from the Queen was a commiserating attitude and a complete refusal to interfere. Besides, the Cardinal had already taken care to provide the Queen with a replacement: the previous Papal Nuncio, Giulio Mazarin.

Six years ago he had presented Mazarin to Anne with the remarkable comment: 'Your Majesty will doubtless approve of this sagacious personage; for he, an agent of His Holiness, bears, as you perceive, a strong resemblance to the late Lord Buckingham.' Later on, when Mazarin had rendered important assistance to France in its relations with Rome, Richelieu offered him a more advantageous position in his own service, and soon the clever and subtle Italian became his most trusted adviser. The Cardinal was so impressed by Mazarin's cleverness and political dexterity, that he even began to train him as his possible successor when his own health was declining. Now, recommending him as a confidential counsellor to Anne, he achieved his purpose absolutely. In her loneliness Anne soon fell under the spell of this handsome and romantic man, who spared no effort in flattering her self-esteem and her vanity.

Having thus taken care of both Louis and Anne, Richelieu had no longer any wish to see Mme de Chevreuse back in France. Marie was left in despair in Dunkirk. She did not want to return to England, where the civil war was continuing, and have to live on the charity of King Charles as a pitiful hanger-on at a court which was itself in difficulties. The King of Spain and the powerful minister Olivarez wrote inviting her to come to Madrid; but she had continually repeated that she had only fled through Spain as there was no other possible way out of France. If she went there now she would be declared a traitor, all her possessions would be confiscated and she would never be able to return to her family. So she decided to defy fate and go to Brussels, which, though it belonged to Spain, was the asylum for French refugees from Richelieu's oppression.

In spite of her forty years, Marie must have retained much of her charm, because immediately the gossip started that the warm welcome which she received from the Governor of the Spanish Netherlands, with sumptuous fêtes given in her honour, was due to the fact that he had fallen in love with her, and with his help she soon re-established her influence completely. When preliminary talks about the possibility of formal peace negotiations failed because Richelieu was more and more demanding, and the Spanish attitude, in the beginning very conciliatory, hardened, the Cardinal used her presence in Brussels as an excuse, writing to Louis that no tolerable peace could be hoped for at present, as Mme de Chevreuse had given the Spaniards such an adverse description of the situation in France that they would not conclude any treaty on reasonable terms. This accusation was no more than a threadbare attempt to exonerate himself for his failure to enforce his demands, because all he could say about the disclosures by Mme de Chevreuse to the Spaniards was:

'A sick monarch, weary of the war; an invalid Prime Minister, who also has only a short time to live; and when both, the sovereign and his minister, have passed away, the return of all the exiles, which would make France a prey to disorder.'

There was certainly no need of any effort on the part of Mme de Chevreuse to inform the Spaniards of these universally known facts, but Richelieu was aware that the mention of her as the cause of his failure was always certain to make an impression on Louis. In reality, her activity in Brussels was much more practical. She had found her old friend Charles of Lorraine there as a helpless refugee and immediately set about convincing him that he was wasting his time. Just now, as the war was still being fought, France needed every ally she could get in the neighbouring lands such as Lorraine. Instead of sitting in Brussels as a refugee he would be well advised to take advantage of the opportunity and come to terms with Richelieu.

He followed her directions and applied for a safe-conduct to travel to Paris. He received it and his petition for his reinstatement as the Duke of Lorraine was granted after he had paid homage to Louis. Although he lost some towns which were to be united with France and his capital Nancy had to endure a French garrison as long as the war lasted, he could return home as the ruler of his country, though with the obligation to assist the King with his troops whenever required.

Marie's next action was indeed of quite a different nature. The rebellious cousin of Louis, the Comte de Soissons, who had fled from Richelieu's persecution to Sedan, an independent fortress belonging to the Duc de Bouillon, was making it a centre for active conspiracy. Richelieu forbade Bouillon to harbour him any longer and ordered Soissons to retire to Venice, but both refused to obey and started to prepare for civil war. Soissons summoned from the capital a nephew of the Archbishop of Paris, the 26-year-old Abbé Paul de Gondi, later the Cardinal de Retz, who was already known as a restless and ambitious propagandist whose fiery speeches excited the populace, and charged him with preparing an insurrection in the capital itself, which was to break out after the first success of the rebels. To gain Spanish support Soissons also sent an envoy, Alexander de Campion, to Mme de Chevreuse in Brussels. She was naturally eager to provide help for a revolt against Richelieu, wrote to Olivarez in Madrid, and received a promise of assistance from the Spanish Governor in Brussels. She helped the envoy to recruit mercenaries and to find officers for them; however, she advised caution and very careful preparation before starting any action. But the impetuous Soissons was not to be restrained.

When Louis declared him, as well as the other conspirators, enemies of the State, Soissons replied with a manifesto against Richelieu, branding him as the cause of all the evil which was ruining the country and troubling the whole of Christendom, and called the French nobles and the people to join him and revolt against the Cardinal's despotism. Altogether he assembled about 10,000 men. The royal army which Louis had sent into Champagne was of about equal strength, but as Charles of Lorraine on his reinstatement had undertaken the duty to assist the King with his troops when requested, he was called in to reinforce the blockade of Sedan. Charles failed to appear, the rebels crossed the Meuse and in the ensuing battle the royal troops were beaten. Louis and Richelieu, who had been in Picardy, hastened with all troops available to Paris, when suddenly the news reached them that Soissons, just after his victory, had mysteriously been shot in the head and was dead. With his death the rebellion collapsed and Campion, his envoy to Mme de Chevreuse, wrote to her that he fully believed in her grief over the death of the Count, which was shared by thousands of unhappy men who had now lost all hope of relief, and 'she was the first person whom the Cardinal would like to ruin'. Yet the immediate action of Louis and Richelieu was to take revenge on Charles for his breach of promise, and four months after his reinstatement the French troops reoccupied Lorraine and forced him to abdicate.

The Cardinal seemed triumphant in every direction. Nevertheless his mood is reflected by an entry in his diary: 'It is easier to control the battlefields of Europe than the four square yards of His Majesty's study.' The King was completely infatuated with Cinq-Mars: he had loaded the youth with costly gifts; he had even conferred on him the exalted post of Grand Equerry, which implied the intimate friendship and confidence of the King; but Cinq-Mars was far from returning the King's affection and started to hate his pastimes, such as gardening, making toys and cooking sweets. When he had to accompany Louis to St Germain he rode nearly every night to Paris, to some ladies of the Court with whom he had love affairs, and when he returned tired, quarrels broke out between him and Louis, and each time Richelieu had to play the arbiter, to reconciliate, and to draw up solemn peace treaties which were just as quickly broken. The Cardinal's reminders to Cinq-Mars that he had been given his job in order to make himself useful were in vain. In his conceit the young man demanded from the King that he be admitted to the State Council and finally accompanied him to a Council meeting, whereupon Richelieu brushed aside all important affairs which were due to be dealt with and spent the duration of the meeting on trivial details, remarking that State affairs could not be discussed before children.

From that moment Cinq-Mars became a deadly enemy of the Cardinal and began to persuade the King that he was suffering intolerable tyranny and abuse which would never end so long as Richelieu lived. As some other courtiers had already discovered, Louis now listened with pleasure to accusations against his chief minister who had once been so humble in his attitude before the King but now relentlessly imposed his will upon his royal master. Louis suffered the yoke with distaste but felt unable to cope himself with the problems that arose continuously and knew of no one else who could successfully deal with them. Although Richelieu's promise – to raise his, the King's, name throughout Europe to 'the point which was rightfully due to him' – still held good but forced him to endure what he felt as a personal humiliation, he drew a kind of satisfaction from hearing from other favourites passionate criticism of the man whom he had periodically to assure of his undiminished favour and regard. He refrained only from saying anything himself which could be construed as approval of their opinions and be brought to the knowledge of the Cardinal by his spies.

Thus Cinq-Mars could continue with his attacks, and as he heard neither approval nor disapproval from the King he began to put his plans into practice. Through his friends he approached the opponents of Richelieu's regime and drew them in. If a coalition could be firmly established to make a united stand against the ailing Cardinal, it would create a centre of resistance which could be difficult to overcome. But just as Soissons had not had the patience to wait, so Cinq-Mars and his collaborators were in an even greater hurry, afraid not only that the King's grace might not endure but also that Richelieu's spies might uncover the conspiracy. They therefore decided to approach Spain. Soon the conditions for a treaty were agreed; Spain was prepared to provide the necessary money and 17,000 men to join the conspirators. As one could not be sure of the King, Gaston was to take over the throne, but strictly as regent for Anne and the Dauphin. The territory which had been taken by the small French conquests on the frontier was to be given back, and an alliance between the royal Catholic houses of France and Spain was to be formed.

At this time Richelieu's troops were engaged in an attack on the frontier town of Perpignan, and the King and the Cardinal decided to go there. Before his departure from St Germain, Louis proved once more that his aversion to Anne and his distrust of her had not abated; he forbade her to leave St Germain in his absence, or even to visit Paris or any convent, or to carry on any foreign correspondence – which naturally meant with Mme de Chevreuse, thus proving that he did not believe in the sincerity of her gesture on receipt of Marie's letter. As the three-year-old Dauphin was frightened and shied away when the King came into the room in his armour, he immediately accused Anne of trying to train the boy to hate him and ordered that the children were to remain strictly in the care of their nurse, who was a relative of the Cardinal, threatening that in the case of disobedience the children would be taken away to Vincennes and remain there until his return.

Then he departed with Richelieu, Cinq-Mars and the usual attendants. During the long journey the already ailing Cardinal broke down completely at Narbonne. His whole body was covered with boils and he could scarcely move. In order to have the King to himself Cinq-Mars persuaded Louis to continue the journey and they proceeded to Roussillon, while Richelieu had himself carried to Tarascon. Alone, in terrible pain and with scarcely any hope of recovery he had already dictated his last will when he unexpectedly received – it has never been established from whom – a copy of the treaty made between the conspirators and Spain. Some of his contemporaries believed that it had passed through Anne's hands, others that a spy, a Spanish monk, had brought it to him. This surprising document revived him. Though his arm was so ulcerated that he could scarcely hold a pen, he wrote a letter to the King drawing a frightful picture of the difficulties, of the dangers menacing not only the allies of France, such as the Prince of

Orange, but the whole of the French realm, claiming that the Queen-Mother and Mme de Chevreuse were already preparing for their return to France. He sent Chancellor Chavigny to Roussillon with this letter and a copy of the treaty.

Louis in Roussillon was also ill with an attack of enteritis. His reaction to Richelieu's letter was to order the immediate arrest of all persons mentioned in the treaty, even including Gaston, and then he took upon himself the humiliating task of travelling to Tarascon and of being carried to the Cardinal's bed-chamber, where he had to confess that he had known at least of Cinq-Mars' feelings towards the Cardinal, but pretended that he had only listened in order to discover the young man's intentions. He gave Richelieu absolute power over the fate of all the men arrested and appointed him Lieutenant-General of the Kingdom. Then he left Tarascon and travelled by slow stages back to St Germain.

Richelieu was again omnipotent in France, but his sickness was thought to be mortal and the question was only how long he could survive. Under these circumstances the mood of the Court was uncertain. When Chancellor Chavigny arrived in Paris and went to pay his respects to Queen Anne at St Germain, she expressed her joy at the failure of the conspiracy and enquired about the Cardinal's intentions. She asked Chavigny to assure him that 'she was resolved to follow his instructions in all matters'; and then she began speaking of the rumours circulating that the relatives and friends of Mme de Chevreuse had petitioned the Cardinal to allow her to return to France because she had no means of subsistence in Brussels. And as the news had just arrived of the death of the Queen-Mother in Cologne, in such poverty that she had to burn her furniture to heat her room, it was said that the Cardinal intended to be lenient.

In his report about this conversation Chavigny wrote:

'The Queen has earnestly enquired of me if it were true that Mme de Chevreuse is returning, and, without awaiting my answer, she explained to me that she would be very grieved at seeing her in France at present; that she knew her for what she was; and she ordered me to request Your Eminence, on her behalf, that, if you had any desire to do something for Mme de Chevreuse, that it would be done without permitting her to return to France. I assured Her Majesty that she would be satisfied on this point.'

Was Anne's extraordinary attitude in the summer of 1642, after Louis' recent prohibition of communication with Mme de Chevreuse and Anne's own confinement to St Germain, simply a ruse to dispel the King's and Richelieu's suspicions; or did she have a new favourite among the crowd of courtiers who, with the declining health of the King, began to converge around Anne, and was she really afraid of Marie's sarcastic tongue?

A fortnight later Chavigny wrote again:

'Never have I seen a more true or more sincere satisfaction than that which the Queen has shown on learning what I said on behalf of Monseigneur. She protests that not only is she unwilling for Mme de Chevreuse to approach her, but that she is resolved, for her own safety, to suffer no one to counsel her to do the least thing contrary to her duty.'

Whatever her motive was, the Cardinal had neither the time nor the inclination to waste his energies on such considerations. In fact, nobody had recently made any appeal to him on behalf of Mme de Chevreuse. Besides, his thoughts were fully occupied with the difficulties of his impending return to the capital. This journey became a procession such as had never been seen before. As every motion of the horse-drawn carriage on the rough roads caused him insufferable pain, he had a portable wooden chamber built with enough room inside for his bed, a table for the secretary, and a couch. This travelling house was placed on a barge for the journey up the River Rhône to Lyons. From there it was carried by sixteen men along the road to Roanne, where it was placed on another barge on the River Loire. Lodgings were prepared for the Cardinal every night in the next town on the route. Where the town gates were too narrow for the passage of the litter, adjoining parts of the city wall were demolished. The windows of the house designed as his lodging were taken out and the wall between them broken down to provide space for his accommodation. At each town a deputation of the municipal authorities waited to welcome him, the town bells rang and the banner of the Cardinal was flown side by side with the French flag.

During this extraordinary procession he wrote to the King, informing him of the execution of Cinq-Mars and the friend who had played the part of go-between, notifying Louis at the same time of the fall of Perpignan to the French. Against the arrested Gaston an edict was being prepared which would deprive him and his descendants for ever of the right of succession to the French throne in the event of the extinction of the royal line. But such an edict required the sanction of the Council of State and of the Parlement before it could be made effective, and Richelieu had therefore to wait until the end of his journey.

When he arrived in Rueil, Louis came to visit him. Anne, too, came with him and brought the little Dauphin, whom he embraced. But his whole attitude was not yet that of a man resigned to his fate. On the contrary, he made increasing claims which Louis found insolent and which made him feel that he was being ordered about, as if he were not the King but a subordinate to his Minister. It sometimes needed all the diplomatic suavity of Mazarin, for whom Richelieu had obtained the Cardinal's hat, to soothe the King's sensibility.

Thus a whole month passed before Louis agreed to go and see the Cardinal again after his arrival in Paris, and finally he went only when he was told that his Minister was dying and pleading for a last interview. On the entrance of the King all the officials thronging the room withdrew, and for some time the two men were left alone. When the King came out again, it was observed that he strolled leisurely through the rooms of the palace, attentively looking at the magnificent pictures on the walls, and then, satisfied, he returned to the Louvre.

Two days later on December 4, 1642, Richelieu died at the age of fifty-seven years, and when the news was conveyed to the King, who was sitting alone in a chamber of the Louvre overlooking the Seine, he said, after a protracted silence, dismissing the courier with a wave of his hand: 'A great statesman is dead.'

Chapter VI

Louis was fully aware that the whole country had regarded everything that had been happening in France as Richelieu's work and that he himself was considered to be merely a figurehead, a puppet in the hands of the all-powerful Minister. To satisfy his own pride and self-esteem, he had now to prove that the whole policy which had been pursued and all the decisions which had been made were his own. Everyone was to see that he had always been the ruler and that the Cardinal had merely been executing his orders; therefore Richelieu's death did not change anything. Accordingly all ministers were confirmed in their offices and the letters which went out to the governors of every province informed them that the policy of the Government remained the same. The petitioners who came rushing from all sides in the hope of appointments and offices, or to plead for some of the Cardinal's victims, were repulsed with the warning that anybody who had 'the impertinence to speak to the King about the banished or imprisoned men, or other villains, was running the danger of finding himself in the Bastille.'

At first Louis actually attended personally to the daily affairs of government, and this occupation blunted a little the feeling of solitude into which Richelieu had put him by isolating him more and more as the years had gone by, and by cutting him off from all normal, friendly contacts. But the business of government alone could not satisfy Louis' feelings and the realization of his own loneliness grew. Most of the companions of his younger days were either wandering somewhere in Europe or rotting behind stone walls. Men who could have been dangerous to the crown had perished in any case: the Cardinal had sent four dukes, five counts, a marshal of France and a royal equerry to the scaffold, and when Louis now gave his thoughts free rein, he felt that some of the numerous prisoners could be released and some of the exiles pardoned without in any way diminishing the dignity of the crown. Thus he began to issue letters of pardon. The Dukes of Vendôme and Guise were allowed to return; the Marshals of Bassompierre and Vitry were set free, and some other high nobles pardoned. Thus the picture of a less rigorous and less despotic rule began to emerge. A milder atmosphere seemed to prevail; better, less anxious days were dawning, and St Germain once more became the centre for the members of the high nobility. The houses of the nobles in Paris, closed because of their owners' exile, reopened and were again blazing with lights.

But while many of the refugees could now return to France, Marie had to remain in Brussels without any prospect of rejoining her family. It was in vain that in January 1643 Marie wrote to the Duc de Chevreuse:

'I beg you to prepare the way for my return by your own and your friends' efforts, without even bringing the Queen into the affair, but simply representing that fear alone caused me to leave France, since up to that time I had remained very patiently in Touraine, and should never have quitted it as I did save for that; that my inclination has always been to esteem the person of the King and to have more confidence in him than in anyone else in the world; that my misfortune and the craft of my enemies have at length reduced me to the situation in which I am, but that I shall retain until death the obligation and inclination which I have to honour and serve the King; that I do not wish to importune him, and that he will do me the favour not to believe anything to the contrary. With this I shall remain content, being well assured that one day he will understand my true sentiments. You must find means of telling him this, but without pressing anything further until we see more clearly that the ministers are favourably disposed.'

Although Marie had now been in exile for nearly six years there was no question of including her in any act of pardon. The King's hatred of Mme de Chevreuse was generally known, and it seemed that this hatred was growing, for in his talks with his nearest collaborators Louis himself repeatedly spoke of her 'with great agitation, stressing the confusion and unhappiness which she had brought to all with whom she had ever come into contact.' Thus, if the rumours that Richelieu had intended to do something to alleviate her position had any foundation, his death extinguished any such hope.

It was said that the dying Cardinal had put before the King three demands: that Mazarin should become his chief adviser, that the command of the army against Spain should be given to the son of Condé (the young Duc d'Enghien whom the Cardinal had married off to one of his nieces), and that Gaston should be excluded for ever from holding a position of authority in the kingdom. The first two demands were immediately met; however, instead of ratifying the decree against Gaston and his descendants, which Richelieu had drafted, Louis ordered the preparation of a new edict making his brother Lieutenant-General of France and entrusting him with the regency during the minority of the Dauphin.

Although no more than forty-two years of age, the King felt that his strength was rapidly failing, and this edict was meant to prevent any risk of civil war after his death. Moreover, the position of Regent would otherwise traditionally belong to Anne, and Louis' distrust of her was as acute as ever. When the members of the State Council pointed out that his order infringed the customary rights of a Queen, he replied: 'You do not know the Queen; you condemn the evils which arose during the regency of Our revered mother; do you want Our kingdom to be exposed to still worse dangers?'

But when the final decision had to be taken he could not completely exclude the mother of the Dauphin from the Government, and the edict which was eventually worked out appointed a Regency Council to rule the country. It was to govern by a plurality of votes. Any change in the membership of the Council, any diminution or increase in their numbers for any reason or under any pretext whatever was forbidden. In accordance with tradition, Anne should have the title: Regent of France, but the President of the Council was to be Gaston, and in his absence the old Prince de Condé, who as a Bourbon was the next in the line of succession to the throne. None of the orders of the 'Queen Regent' was to be considered valid or legal without the sanction of the Council, and if any of the great offices fell vacant the Queen was to fill it only as advised by and with the consent of the Council.

By the creation of such an immutable Regency Council, Louis thought that he had ensured the continuation of the present government. The real power in the Council would be in the hands of Mazarin, of the Chancellor, of the Secretary of Finance and the Secretary of State, all of whom had been appointed by Richelieu and who continued in their old offices. Although Anne would carry the title of Regent, she would have no power. She could not decide anything, not confer the smallest office in the realm or give any monetary grant to a favourite. Although he made Gaston President of the Council and gave him the highest title in the realm, Louis nevertheless took the precaution of inserting a declaration that in the event of his rebellion against any ordinance issued by the Council he would be deprived of the office of Lieutenant-General and everyone would be forbidden to take orders from him. That meant that he, too, would be completely bound by the majority of the votes in the Council. It was also a precaution against the ambitions of Gaston's followers, who again voiced the opinion that after the death of the King he should declare Anne's children illegitimate and demand the crown for himself.

This decree seemed to Louis to provide a cast-iron safeguard for the continuance of the system of government as he envisaged it, but before the document could be submitted to Parlement for ratification it had to bear Anne's signature, since it determined her position after the King's death. The difficult task of getting her consent to the severe restrictions was entrusted to Mazarin. By this choice Louis proved that he was completely unaware of the motives and intentions of his closest collaborators.

In his confidential talks Mazarin obtained Anne's agreement to the conditions that deprived her of all power by giving a firm promise that the decree would never come into force, but that it had to be signed and registered because it was the most the King would concede, and her refusal could only lead to immediate drastic measures against her. Thus Anne declared herself prepared to obey the King's order, to sign the declaration in his presence and to take the solemn oath to maintain the enactment, although outwardly, to her ever-growing number of adherents, she continued to pretend that Mazarin was her enemy, just as Richelieu had been, and accused him of having influenced the King to stipulate such conditions. Louis, again, was not in the least deceived by her submissive attitude and when, after taking the oath, she thanked him for awarding her the title of Queen-Regent and wanted to kiss his hand, he drew his hand away.

The whole decree was a lengthy document, mentioning in detail all the people who were to receive the King's pardon, how far the pardon was to go, and how the different reinstatements in honours and positions were to be applied. Only two people were completely excluded from any clemency: Mme de Chevreuse and Châteauneuf, the previous Keeper of the Great Seal, who, because of his attachment to her, had acted disloyally. The King's hatred towards Marie did not abate for a moment, the more so because of his fear that after his death she would dominate everyone. As even Richelieu could only be prevented by a special royal prohibition from going to see her, although he knew of the King's sentiments and had his order to banish her, who would be there to withstand her influence?

She had to be kept away from France as long as possible, and so the royal declaration of April 21, 1643 contained the following clause:

'And, inasmuch as for weighty reasons, important for the welfare of our service, we have been obliged to deprive the Sieur de Châteauneuf of the charge of Keeper of the Seals of France, and to cause him to be conducted to the Château of Angoulême, where, in accordance with our orders, he has remained up to the present time, we wish and intend that the said Sieur de Châteauneuf shall remain in the said Château of Angoulême until peace be concluded and executed, provided, notwithstanding, that he may not be set at liberty, save by the order of the said Regent, with the advice of the said Council, who shall appoint a place of his retirement within or without the kingdom, as shall be judged best. And, as our intention is to provide against every matter which may in any way trouble the good arrangements which we are making for the peace and tranquillity of our State, the knowledge that we have of the injurious conduct of the Duchesse de Chevreuse, and of the artifices which she has employed up to the present time to foment division in our realm, and the factions and the intelligence which she maintains with our enemies without, makes us judge it advisable to forbid, as we have in fact forbidden her, entry into our realm so long as the

8. Anne of Austria, from a painting at Versailles

9. Louis XIII, from a portrait by Ph. de Champaigne

war continues; desiring also that, after peace be concluded and executed, she may not return into our realm save by permission of the Queen-Regent, given with the sanction of the Council. If such permission be conceded, we desire that the royal grace shall be vouchsafed only on the condition that the said Duchess never approaches the Court or the person of the said Queen-Regent.'

When the document, complete in every detail, was brought to the King and read aloud paragraph by paragraph before its presentation to Parlement, Louis was lying immobile, listening with closed eyes, but when the reader came to the passage about Mme de Chevreuse he, as the courtiers present afterwards recounted, opened his eyes and, raising his emaciated hand with one finger outstretched, exclaimed in a croaking voice: 'This woman is the devil! She is the devil! The very devil!'

The decree went before the Parlement of Paris and was obediently registered and became law. Now everyone awaited the peaceful death of the King; but he still lingered on for three weeks while the courtiers clustered around him all the time in discomfort, afraid to leave St Germain in case Louis recovered from his attack of enteritis, as he had done so often before, and observed their absence.

At last, on May 14, 1643, Louis XIII died in the presence of the Queen, his brother Gaston, the Prince de Condé and all the great lords of the realm, and now, relieved, they all rushed to Paris. His death promised a still more fundamental change than did the death of Richelieu six months earlier, because now there was nobody left at the top to maintain the autocratic regime. Anne had always been a subject for comment and compassion in Court circles. She was pitied for the cruel treatment meted out to her, and even if she had really maintained some kind of correspondence with Madrid and Brussels, it was after all only to her own brothers that she was said to have been writing, and many nobles and courtiers, not to mention the ecclesiastics, condemned the fratricidal war between the two Catholic powers. Now, five days after the King's death, the young d'Enghien won a decisive battle at Rocroi against the Spanish forces, and when the news of the great victory reached the capital, solemn thanksgiving services were held everywhere in the expectation that the new government would bring about an honourable peace and give a respite to the exhausted country.

The question of the form of the new government naturally occupied everyone's thoughts, but the idea of the Regency Council as devised by Louis XIII was universally disliked. Even the men chosen by him to preside over it did not relish the prospect of high-sounding titles without being given any power to influence the decisions which would in effect be made by the majority of ministers in the permanent Council while the odium for any unpopular actions would fall upon them. Therefore, when shortly after the news of d'Enghien's victory a solemn session of Parlement took place, at first Gaston and then Condé expressed their agreement to the revocation of Louis' decree, and the same Parlement which through its ratification had made it law a couple of weeks earlier now revoked it. As Anne had been named Queen-Regent, though without any power, and no one expected her to be able to rule effectively, Omer Talon, the Attorney-General of the High Court, proposed that she should be declared Regent with full control of the administration, while Gaston as Lieutenant-General of the Realm should be President of her Council, but subject to the authority of the Queen. However, as Mazarin had foreseen, the main dissatisfaction was caused by the idea of an irremovable body at the head of the Government, whatever its policy might be; and so it was proposed that the Queen should not have to retain the members of the Council as at present, but be empowered to appoint such persons as ministers whom she deemed worthy and proper. All princes and peers approved the proposal as every faction, considering Anne's inability to govern, saw in this change the possibility of advancement to high positions and power.

Other members of Parlement also welcomed the proposal and did not fail to stipulate, on their part, that 'permission should be given to Parlement to advise on matters pertaining to the welfare of the realm and to pass a vote of censure on the proceedings taken by the late Government'. This provision was accepted, and the members of Parlement, together with the great nobles who had suffered under Richelieu's rule and after his death failed to get any satisfaction from Louis, were confidently looking forward to the establishment of a less tyrannical regime.

Thus all Louis' precautions to exclude Anne from the Government, or at least to deprive her of any real power, proved to have been in vain, and the reversal of the King's policy was expected by all. His ministers would be dismissed and new favourites would receive the Queen's confidence. As a sister of the King of Spain she would come to terms with her brother and put an end to the sanguinary struggle between the country of her birth and that of her adoption. The ministers to whom the continuance of the King's policy had been entrusted were the creatures of Richelieu, who had persecuted her and exiled her friends. Mazarin, the little-known Italian diplomat, who had been Richelieu's protégé and had afterwards been chosen by the late King to continue the old regime in the Regency Council, was generally more despised than hated, and it was said that he was preparing to leave France.

The man who conceived the greatest hopes was the young Duc de Beaufort, a son of the Duc de Vendôme, who had for a long time been particularly attached to the Queen. She had just given him a public mark of esteem by entrusting him, shortly before Louis' death, with the care of the Dauphin and of her second son, the Duc d'Anjou. When she appointed her Great Almoner, the Bishop of Beauvais, as First Minister in her Council, everyone understood that this was purely a prestige appointment for the old man which might bring the blessings of heaven upon her actions. But then came an astonishing blow to all her adherents: she called for Mazarin as her chief adviser and confirmed all the ministers of the previous reign in their positions. When her followers expressed their amazement, her answer was that these men were indispensable for the time being, as they alone held the keys to the affairs of the Government, and the Great Almoner confirmed her judgment by his actions, for he acted purely as a puppet figure, asking the ministers for advice on every decision and following their directions.

Thus it was now to Mazarin that all friends and adherents of the Queen had to apply if they had any requests, and his attitude was pleasantly surprising. In contrast to Richelieu he treated every petitioner with the utmost friendliness; he always seemed to be trying to please and to be of service, and deeply regretted that he was unable to fulfil the desires of an applicant immediately, because the Queen required that all appeals of any kind, whether for grants to returned exiles, or for the reinstatement of the nobility in their old positions, or for anything else, were to be delivered into her own hands, so that she herself could make the decision. However, this subtlety satisfied the applicants in the beginning; they did not see him as an obstacle to their desires until much later, when the falsity of this display became obvious. At first all were quite happy to wait. And they were also waiting impatiently, some with hope, some with dread, for the expected great event of the return of Mme de Chevreuse who, as everybody was certain, would use her influence to give a firm course to this uncertain, fumbling government.

Chapter VII

When Anne had become Queen-Regent with unrestricted power Marie naturally expected an immediate urgent recall to Paris; but the call did not come. Instead, letters from Marie's various friends began to arrive with bewildering descriptions of the Queen's conduct when they had approached her on behalf of Mme de Chevreuse. At first they were given the excuse that as the dying King in his last will had strictly forbidden her return as long as the war lasted, she was afraid of the impression which might be made on the country if the exile were to be recalled straight away. When they replied that the decree had been annulled to give her, the Queen-Regent, full powers they received the answer that she 'no longer had any taste for the amusements which had bound her and Marie together in their youth and that she was concerned to appear to her friend as greatly changed'. Only after long and persistent efforts did they manage to draw out of her the real reason for her refusal to recall Mme de Chevreuse: she was afraid that Marie might 'disturb the peace of her regency', that she would intrigue against Mazarin just as she had done against Richelieu and create endless difficulties for her government. All their representations about the bad impression which would be created if she used her power to keep her friend out of the country, while all the other exiles were allowed to return, failed to achieve anything.

However, the troubles which Anne had feared Marie might create began to develop without any intervention on the part of Mme de Chevreuse. The Queen's devoted adherents, the so-called 'Importants', had begun to exercise their influence at Court, in the salons, in Parlement and even in the provinces. One of their leaders was the young son of the Duc de Vendôme, the proud Duc de Beaufort, to whom Anne had entrusted the care of her two sons, and he, with his collaborators and friends, was not prepared to submit to Mazarin's domination. They gathered around them other dissatisfied nobles who wanted to be given honours and positions in accordance with tradition, and this movement alarmed Anne and Mazarin.

Marie's friends took advantage of these apprehensions. They argued that the best way to stabilize the situation was indeed to recall Mme de Chevreuse, who would have the Guise-Lorraine family behind her, and so provide a counterbalance. Her recall had thus become a political issue, and after some vacillation, about three weeks after the death of the King, the Queen sent her the invitation to return to Paris, expressing the hope that Marie would live 'in good understanding' with the Cardinal. Lord Montagu, as his envoy, told her that Mazarin expected 'a cordial friendship to develop between them' and offered her in his name the money she might need to pay off any debts incurred. But this clumsy offer to buy her friendship only made her explode: 'Who is this impudent lackey who dares proffer a bribe to a Rohan!'

This sudden recall, made in these particular circumstances, told Marie that she was needed in Paris, and although her friends warned her not to make any plans before she herself had seen the Queen and ascertained her feelings, so that she could decide on her own future conduct, she set out fully convinced that Anne's posturing had been a blind, a manoeuvre to deceive the people around her and cover up her inability to govern. Marie believed herself able to bring this senseless war to an end, since Anne's brother, Philip IV of Spain, had proposed peace negotiations on advantageous terms and expressed his hope of Marie's support. Charles of Lorraine, once more a helpless refugee, put all his trust in her skill to bring about the evacuation of his duchy for the second time. Henriette-Marie of England cherished the thought that France, freed from the burden and cares of war, would intervene in the dangerous rising against her husband, the King. All these expectations centred around Mme de Chevreuse.

A brilliant procession marked her departure from Brussels. Her coach was followed by twenty other coaches, with the highest nobility of the Spanish Netherlands providing her with a guard of honour for the first part of her journey. At Mons she had to pass the camp of the Spanish army and was saluted by the commander with military honours. Then she proceeded to Cambrai, and on the outskirts of every place and every stronghold on French soil she was welcomed by the governor accompanied by provincial nobles. At Péronne she was greeted by her friend Campion, who had repeatedly warned her about the atmosphere at the Court, and by the Duc de Chaulnes, the brother of Luynes, who had arranged a magnificent reception for her at his château. From there she travelled to Roye, where her loyal friend Marsillac, upon the death of his father the Duc de la Rochefoucauld, awaited her. He told her that he had been specially sent by Anne to impress upon her how much the Court had changed and to make her understand that she must not expect to be able to influence the Queen as before, but to be 'content with the much humbler position in which she would have to remain in future'. He advised her to comply with the wishes of the Queen and to accept any offers of friendship from Mazarin, who as yet had not acted offensively and was seeking 'to gain her support for his interests'. He had shown none of the violence of Richelieu and was, moreover, practically the only person with a complete understanding of foreign policy. But he tried to make her understand that any idea of guiding the Queen as in the old days was out of the question. He wrote about this conversation: 'Mme de Chevreuse promised to follow all my suggestions.'

Did she really mean to keep her promises? He also mentioned that the Queen had instructed him to tell her that such a great parade as her journey had been 'scarcely befitting a returning exile'; on the other hand, the reception given to her everywhere in France was directly due to Mazarin's orders to local officials. So the impression which she got on her way home of the atmosphere of the Court was a contradictory one. At Compiègne the Duc de Chevreuse was waiting for her with a host of high nobles to provide her with an escort of honour to Paris, but he also did not fail to warn Marie as to how much Anne had changed. Yet Marie still did not take the warning seriously.

Her entry into Paris after ten years of absence, six of them spent in exile in foreign countries, was triumphant, with crowds lining the streets through which she passed. The *Gazette*, the official Court circular, published a glowing description of her eight-day journey and her arrival in the capital, concluding the narration with the special compliment to the now 43-year-old Duchesse de Chevreuse:

'But the great retinue of Court nobles who fill her spacious palace to overflowing does not inspire us with so deep an admiration as the fact that the fatigues of her long wanderings, with all the vicissitudes and severity of her fate, have not wrought the smallest change in her natural magnanimity, nor, which is still more extraordinary, in her beauty!'

Yes, she was still beautiful, but her beauty had assumed a different character. The impulsive, impish mischief of her youth, expressed in her looks and her whole behaviour, had now been replaced by purpose and determination without impairing her wit, which remained as incisive as ever, or her zest for life, which still animated her lively features and made men admire her. Now she was back in Paris, in her home, surrounded by friends, old and new, all expecting some kind of political action from her, and she was preparing to show them that neither her vigour nor her abilities had suffered in the slightest from her hardships.

When she went to the Louvre to pay homage to Anne, she found her old friend to be changed still more. The Queen no longer retained any trace of the wistful creature who had made one eager to help and to serve her. She had become a portly figure with imperiously flashing eyes and, at the slightest hint of opposition, a shrill angry voice, completely impervious to any suggestions. Her every word had to be law. After a few short welcoming and polite phrases of a general nature she shocked Marie with the instruction that 'as the allies of France might become suspicious if directly on her return from Flanders she remained at Court in the Queen's entourage, it would be better for her first to make a little journey into the country – to Dampierre'.

Marie's surprise lasted scarcely a moment; then she had the correct answer ready: she was naturally prepared to obey, but might it not be useful if 'the Queen were to recollect that the whole of Europe knew how she had been persecuted for her love of, and her allegiance to Her Majesty and that Her Majesty might do an injury to her own reputation by sending her away the moment she had arrived'.

Mazarin was, of course, present at the reception and she asked Anne to consult him. He had constantly warned Anne that Mme de Chevreuse would return determined to induce her to desert the honourable allies of the crown, and prepared to ruin the realm and detract from the Queen's popularity. But now that she was here and he had assured her of his hope for a fruitful collaboration, he could not very well advise the Queen in her presence to demand her departure. Thus Marie's quick-witted reply had the desired effect. She remained in Paris as the friend of the Queen, with easy access to the Louvre, while the Hôtel de Chevreuse became the meeting place for all factions of the nobility. Marie lost no time in acquainting herself with the various aspects of the situation.

The 'Importants', who in the last months of the reign of Louis had surrounded Anne as her supporters and friends, expected to be reinstated in the positions of which they had been deprived by Richelieu, and their leaders, especially the Vendômes, the illegitimate descendants of Henri IV, counted on Marie's friendship and her help in influencing the Queen. Mazarin, on his part, pursuing the policy of Richelieu but feeling himself in a much weaker position, lost no opportunity in endeavouring to win Mme de Chevreuse to his cause. To present her with 80,000 livres on behalf of the Queen he visited her himself and enquired as to her wishes and ideas. With the Court divided into two hostile parties Marie well understood her chances and at first tried to lessen the tension. To Mazarin's enquiries she replied that for herself she did not want anything. Her only desire was to eradicate the injustices which Richelieu had committed. The Vendômes had been the governors of Brittany when Richelieu induced the King to arrest and imprison the Duc without any trial and had given the province to one of his own relatives. Did justice not demand the Duc's reinstatement? Again, La Rochefoucauld had always been a supporter of Anne's cause and had therefore been kept out of office; would it not be just if the Queen were now to recompense him, perhaps with the governorship of Le Havre, which was being ruled in the name of a nephew of Richelieu, still a minor?

Mazarin professed his friendship and his wish to be of help; he would see what could be done. But he fully understood what these demands for justice implied: they meant the undoing of Richelieu's work of crushing the power of the semi-independent nobility. Vendôme in the possession of Brittany, with La Rochefoucauld in Le Havre, would mean delivering north-western France into the hands of these unreliable nobles, who were always prepared to resist any encroachment of the Government. Had Mme de Chevreuse already joined his adversaries? In any case, he immediately advised Anne to take over the government of Brittany nominally herself. That meant the man in command there would be acting only as her deputy, and such a position was beneath the dignity of the princes of the royal blood.

Moreover, he had taken care to win to his side the other prince of Bourbon blood, Condé, who had always been the enemy of the Vendômes, by restoring to him all possible privileges and grants. As the father of d'Enghien, the victor of Rocroi, who was naturally eager for more military glory and advancement, Condé also desired the war against Spain to continue. Nevertheless, the nervousness at Court about Marie's activity is shown by Mazarin's entry in his diary, 'Great efforts are being made to reconcile Condé with the house of Vendôme', and he reveals his lack of confidence even in his near collaborator by continuing: 'Condé has said that it would be expedient to sow mistrust between Her Majesty and myself and to make her believe that I am devoted to Monsieur [Gaston] and desire to make him Co-regent!'

Gaston, the brother of the dead King, Lieutenant-General of the Realm and confirmed by Parlement as President of the Regency Council, was the only person of whose attitude both sides were uncertain, because as always nobody knew what his decision on any question was likely to be. Mazarin's position was completely dependent on the hold which he had won over Anne. He had ingratiated himself by ecstatically praising her wisdom and her regal qualities and raised her self-esteem by flattering and admiring her. This attitude of the handsome Italian, a year or so younger than herself, whose resemblance to Buckingham had already been drawn to her attention by Richelieu, could not fail to touch her heart. His avowal that, as a foreigner without any family support, he was entirely dependent upon her favour and that he had no other design in life than to serve her, bore fruit. She felt herself just as much a foreigner as he; they conversed with each other in Spanish; no other man could be so trustworthy a friend and adviser; so she fell in love with him, and it came about that after the Council meetings the two alone held conferences until late at night 'for the purpose of instructing the Queen in State affairs'.

122

These conferences became a Court scandal at once. Everyone spoke of them. Anne's pious friends, the abbesses of the convent of Val-de-Grâce and of the Carmelite order, besought the Queen to consider her reputation, but the only result was to make her declare furiously that, if such slanders were repeated, she would never again visit their convents. Various bishops and old friends, who had retired into monasteries, came out specially to warn her that 'midnight conferences of a beautiful woman in her early forties with a man of forty could not be indulged in with impunity'. But these reminders only raised her anger against the 'Devouts' whom she already regarded as a nuisance, because, under the influence of Rome, the leaders of the clergy were also working towards the end of the impious war between France and Spain.

There is no historical evidence that Mazarin was her lover or, as later reports even assert, secretly married to her. The early entries in his notebook show that in the beginning he even distrusted her, for he wrote: 'They say that Her Majesty is the greatest hypocrite living, that no one can place any confidence in her, that if she seems to set any value on somebody it is from sheer necessity.' But later on, when he had an attack of jaundice, we find a note: 'Jaundice, fruit of extreme love.'

The nightly private sessions of instruction continued, and Marie realized that the efforts of the 'Importants' to create discord between Anne and Mazarin were obviously doomed to failure. As her own attempt to win Mazarin's collaboration had been in vain, she was looking for other ways to achieve a change in the government's policy. In Louis' edict the only person besides herself excluded from any royal clemency had been Châteauneuf. However, since the purpose of his disloyalty was to find out the King's and Richelieu's intentions concerning Anne, Mazarin had, after the death of Louis, released him from imprisonment at Angoulême, but only on condition that he retired to his country seat at Montrouge, and on the understanding that he was not to appear at Court until further orders of the Regent. If Châteauneuf could be brought into the government he was the man to challenge Mazarin's supremacy, and so, to Anne, Marie started to praise Châteauneuf's abilities, his knowledge of politics, of matters of state and foreign affairs. But Mazarin immediately intervened by declaring that he would under no circumstances suffer Châteauneuf's return to the Government, and by presenting to the Queen all the troubles and annoyances 'to which she would expose herself if Châteauneuf were to resume his position in the Council'. Knowing the hatred of the Princesse de Condé for Châteauneuf, because of the death sentence which he had obtained against her brother, the Duc de Montmorency, he also set the Condés to influence Anne against Mme de Chevreuse.

His notes were now full of accusations against her: 'This Chevreuse woman, with her thousand cunning ways, must be removed at any price, otherwise she will ruin France!' For her nobles he had only contempt: 'She animates them all. She works to strengthen the Vendômes, she endeavours to win over the whole House of Lorraine, she has already won the Duc de Guise. She has a clear perception of everything and is never discouraged. She asks for only three months in which to show what she can do,' and he does not cease to impress upon Anne that Marie was striving to dominate her.

Recognizing his enmity, and noticing Anne's increasing resentment against any of her suggestions and opinions, Marie understood that the only way to resist the newly developing dictatorial rule was to create such a strong united front of the nobility that the Government would be forced to take note of their views. She now had her daughter Charlotte living with her, a sixteen-year-old beauty, to whom she had given birth in exile in Lorraine. Her other daughters had become nuns, and she had the idea to arrange a marriage between Charlotte and a son of Vendôme, whose other son was due to marry the daughter of the Duc d'Epernon, another great feudal baron, lately also in opposition to the regime. As a daughter of Vendôme had just recently married into a branch of the independent house of Savoy, this would make a combination of four great families with all their adherents. But as soon as he heard rumour of this plan, Mazarin convinced Anne that the union of Vendôme and Savoy would be a menace to the crown, and she forbade the intended marriages.

In order to secure an ally at least for the inauguration of peace talks, Marie tried to interest Gaston in the idea by promising to arrange the marriage of his daughter by his first wife to the Spanish Viceroy in Brussels as soon as peace was achieved. As she had expected, Gaston was very interested; but again under the influence of Mazarin, Anne declared that she would never permit this marriage to take place.

The war must go on. The impoverished, exhausted country had to maintain six armies in Flanders, Germany, Lombardy and Catalonia, and to provide subsidies for its allies Sweden and Holland. That could only be done by a continual increase in taxation. Everybody knew that this policy was Mazarin's, while the falsity of his friendship and sympathetic behaviour had by now also been recognized and hatred of him grew.

Eventually rumours began to circulate of a plot to assassinate him. Suspicious persons armed with daggers or even pistols had been observed lingering in the streets or at inns around the Hôtel de Clèves, where he lived and from where he went every evening in his coach to the Louvre to visit the Queen, returning rather late, accompanied only by a favourite page. Under cover of night an ambush could easily be laid without arousing suspicion, and the only obstacle to its success would be the guards on duty in front of the Queen's palace, who might interfere to protect the Cardinal, since it was only a short distance from the Louvre to the Hôtel de Clèves. But, although the route of his coach and the time when it was usually expected to pass were generally known, no attempt was ever made to attack him. Instead, more rumours were noised abroad, this time naming persons in the plot, at the centre of which, it was said, was the Duc de Beaufort, who had been Anne's favourite and Mazarin's opponent, as well as Mme de Chevreuse towards whom Mazarin's hostility had increased of late. As he noted at the time:

'Mme de Chevreuse inspires them all. She says that, if they do not decide to get rid of me, affairs will not go well; that the great nobles will be quite as much in subjection as before, that my power will continually increase, and that it is necessary to hasten matters before the Duc d'Enghien returns from the army.'

More and more names were mentioned as being implicated in the conspiracy, and finally the precise date was given on which the assassination was to take place. On that day Mazarin ostentatiously forebore to leave his palace, and next morning when rumours started to circulate that the plan had been frustrated, Anne declared to her ladies-in-waiting: 'Before twenty-four hours have passed, you will see how I will avenge myself for this enterprise, devised by such wicked and perfidious friends!'

Was the whole idea of the plot just Mazarin's trick to consolidate his position or had some chance remarks been exaggerated? Anyway, the next day, at the meeting of the State Council, he said: 'I have decided not to risk my life unnecessarily and become the inglorious victim of ambushes, conspiracies and the wiles of my enemies, who are also the enemies of the realm. Permit me therefore to retire to Rome.' This speech had the desired effect. Anne wept, Condé advised her to refuse to accept his resignation, and the Council ordered the immediate arrest of Beaufort and his adherents.

Beaufort had spent the day hunting in the forest of Anet in the vicinity of his father's castle. Mme de Chevreuse was with other ladies at the Louvre, scoffing at the idle and imbecile rumours which had set 'all Paris by the ears', when Beaufort on his return, as he usually did, came to pay homage to the Queen. He was graciously received; Anne enquired how successful his hunting had been and then retired with Mazarin to the adjoining room. But when Beaufort wished to leave, he was arrested at the door by the Captain of the Bodyguard. Turning to Mme de Chevreuse and Mlle de Hautefort, he said: 'You perceive, Mesdames, that the Queen is arresting me!' Next morning he was transported in one of the Queen's coaches under a strong escort to the prison of Vincennes. Immediately more arrests followed, and so everyone in his group who felt himself endangered fled to Anet, where the Duc de Vendôme, Beaufort's father, gave them refuge.

Anne told Marie that she believed her innocent of murderous designs; but since she never ceased to take part in political intrigue and persisted in making comment on affairs of State which were not her concern, as well as critical remarks about events over which she, the Queen, alone had the right to decide, Marie should forthwith retire to Dampierre without formal leave-taking. It was time for her to enjoy in privacy the pleasures of life in France, she declared, and to avoid a reply Anne instantly left the room. When Mme de Chevreuse later induced the Queen's favourite maid-of-honour to intercede on her behalf, Anne immediately banished the lady from Court.

Thus there was no longer any question of trying to gain the ear of the Queen to achieve changes at Court or in the attitude of the government. One had either to submit, or, if the conditions which had existed before Richelieu's rule were to be restored, when each region could live according to its own customs under its own regent, try to unite the nobility with a view to active resistance. Naturally, Marie did not think of submitting. In Dampierre she had sufficient opportunity to communicate with all her friends and to observe every move at Court. For the moment Mazarin was victorious. He had won all along the line, and it had taken him no more than two and a half months to rid himself of the opposing groups of nobles. All he now needed was to consolidate his position.

His first move was quite unexpected: Châteauneuf was summoned to an audience at the Louvre and made Governor of Touraine. Marie fully understood the meaning of this move: it was to show publicly that the Queen was not forgetting the services rendered to her and that she duly rewarded them, while at the same time transferring the man whom Mazarin regarded as a possible rival to a place far from Paris. With his appointment Châteauneuf received the order to depart at once, without seeing Mme de Chevreuse.

Mazarin's next step was to order all bishops residing in Paris to leave the capital and to go to their various dioceses, and this order included the Bishop of Beauvais, who until then had acted as First Minister in the Queen's Council; thus nobody would be in a position to advise the Queen from the point of view of Rome, and Mazarin alone would have her ear. At the same time Anne summoned Gaston, declaring that she would not tolerate his presence in Paris unless he supported the policy of Mazarin and Condé; but as usual with him, she got no definite commitment and she could not risk making him an enemy. Then she requested La Rochefoucauld to reconcile himself with Mazarin and to break off all contact with Mme de Chevreuse; but from him she received the answer that he remained

'as always, Her Majesty's devoted friend and servant. But Mme de Chevreuse was his friend, too, and had previously been his patroness; she had never done any evil to Her Majesty – which would indeed be a reason for abandoning his friendship – and he therefore prayed Her Majesty to excuse him if he declined to forsake Mme de Chevreuse, because she had been unfortunate enough to displease His Eminence the Cardinal.'

Furious, Anne broke off the audience, and La Rochefoucauld was excluded henceforth from any office or military command. The thought of Mme de Chevreuse in Dampierre so near to the capital continued to make the Queen and Mazarin uneasy; Anne could not forget the daring with which Marie had once travelled in disguise from Dampierre to Paris to see her in the convent. Mazarin, meanwhile, kept her under continuous observation through his spies and received from them reports of the constant comings and goings at Dampierre of numerous people, some probably in disguise. It was certainly on Marie's advice that the friends of Beaufort, who had originally taken refuge at Anet with the Duc de Vendôme, now fled from France. Moreover, she was in direct contact with Lord Goring, the English Ambassador, who as Mazarin maintained, was convinced that a change of government would induce Spain to concede most advantageous peace terms, and France would then be able to help Charles of England against the rebellious Parliamentary forces. So Mme de Chevreuse had to be removed from the vicinity of Paris, and she received the order to retire to her country house between Tours and Anger.

However, all these attempts to reinforce Mazarin's power and ensure the continuity of his policy only increased the general hatred. Everyone commiserated with Beaufort, who was held imprisoned without trial or sentence, just as inconvenient nobles had been imprisoned in Richelieu's day, and a new slogan was coined: 'Richelieu is not dead, he has only changed his age.' And as Anne stood completely behind Mazarin, she got a taste of the prevailing mood on the occasion of one of her drives through the streets of Paris, when her coach was suddenly surrounded by market-women hurling insults at her, and the crowd could only be dispersed by her escort of guards.

Mazarin used this incident to draw her attention to the dangers to which he had constantly to expose himself when driving from the Hotel de Clèves to the Louvre for the Council meetings and asked for permission to move into an annexe of Richelieu's palace, where he had lived during the Cardinal's lifetime, and at the same

Cardinal de Retz, from a portrait by
Ph. de Champaigne

10. Cardinal Mazarin

Charles IV Duke of Lorraine, from a
contemporary print

11. The Grand Condé, from a portrait by Teniers

time to have the meetings transferred to that palace. Anne naturally agreed and it was not long before she also transferred her own household from the Louvre to Richelieu's palace, which then became known as the Palais Royal.

In this way Mazarin obtained direct access to the rooms of the Queen at any time of day or night without having to leave the building.

Chapter VIII

For Marie, to be banished to her remote country estate was a repetition of the situation she had experienced under Richelieu, except that now she had her daughter Charlotte with her. But when she tried as before to resume her old contacts and activities, she very soon realized that this time she was being kept under much stricter observation and surrounded by a tight net of spies. While previously her links with Paris and Anne had been assured by the Queen's devoted attendants, now Anne officially and publicly declared that if any courtier visited Mme de Chevreuse, he could expect the Queen's disfavour, and Mazarin ordered the name of every person she saw to be reported to him at once. Thus fewer and fewer people dared to take the risk.

She had naturally again taken a house in Tours, but the town was also no longer what it was. Her friend, the old Archbishop, was dead; new men occupied the administrative positions, and Marie became more and more isolated. As one of her friends, who lived near Tours, wrote in his memoirs: 'This nearly complete segregation, into which she has fallen through the faithlessness of all those people who were obliged to her for help and friendship or had been connected with her by common interests, has taught me how little trust men of our age deserve.' He confessed his esteem for Mme de Chevreuse and his interest in her, and although he continued to go and see her, he stressed the necessity 'to use all possible care to see that my visits do not arouse any suspicion'.

In spite of all this she nevertheless managed to correspond with whomsoever she wished and to get not only a precise picture of the mood and of events in Paris and the provinces, but also the means to collaborate with her friends in plans for Beaufort's escape. She even received an unofficial envoy from d'Enghien, who, after a recent success on the battlefield, had been assured by Anne that no separate agreement with Spain would bring the war to an inglorious end. This could only be brought about by the incessant intrigues at Court. After his victory, when d'Enghien expected promotion to the position of Commander-in-Chief of all the armies in Flanders, Mazarin, afraid of creating a powerful rival, induced Gaston to lay claim to the post. As Gaston was the senior prince of Bourbon blood as well as Lieutenant-General of the Realm, his request could not be refused. Meanwhile, Mazarin acquired the additional advantage of getting Gaston away from Government activities in Paris for the time being and Gaston himself was able to enjoy the pleasures of having his name associated with the taking of Gravelines although he understood nothing of strategy.

Life at Court in Paris outwardly presented a picture of gaiety, while behind the scenes it was full of personal intrigue and mutual suspicion. Diplomatic talks had started in Münster about the possibility of peace negotiations, but Mazarin put forward such unacceptable conditions that the Spanish envoy wrote to Philip IV in Madrid: 'It would be better for Your Majesty if some stranger were sitting on the throne of France than Your Majesty's sister.' However, Mazarin did not fail to point out to Anne that the refusal of the Spaniards to accept his conditions was the result of inform-ation which Mme de Chevreuse had supplied to them about the state of affairs in France.

In this way he followed Richelieu's example; but while the latter had used it to justify himself before Louis, Mazarin pursued it to increase Anne's animosity towards her old friend, and thereby to prevent any possibility that Mme de Chevreuse might one day again appear at Court. If Marie needed further proof of the implacable hostility towards herself, it came when Henriette-Marie, the Queen of England, sought refuge in France after Cromwell's victory at Marston Moor. As the sister of Louis XIII, the English Queen was naturally welcomed in Paris and given a pension and accommodation in the now empty Louvre; but when she wanted to go to a health resort in the south, she got the necessary permis-sion to travel only on the strict condition that under no circum-stances was she to see or to make any contact with Mme de Chevreuse, for her friendship for Marie was well-known. As Mazarin wrote in his diary: 'Henriette-Marie has no right to make contact with a person who, through her dangerous conduct, has lost the favour of Her Majesty.'

A few months later Marie received an even worse blow. She had fallen ill and her doctor, an Italian, came from Tours to treat her.

Afterwards, when he was driving with Charlotte and two of her girl friends in Charlotte's carriage, the coach was suddenly surrounded by an armed gang of Mazarin's men. The doctor, who was suspected of carrying Marie's letters, was arrested, and the ladies were forced to leave the coach, which was then thoroughly searched. Charlotte herself was menaced with a pistol and cries of 'Kill her!', before finally, as nothing was found, she was allowed to drive home with her companions.

This assault was something which Marie could not pass over in silence. She wrote to Anne, describing the behaviour of the assailants, and asked for protection from any repetition of this attack and 'the brutality which has never been committed on such occasions before. This act is so extraordinary that I trust Your justice will vouchsafe an appropriate apology to my daughter for the offence committed against her and hope that Your kindness will protect us against a repetition of such an occurrence.' Anne did not consider it necessary to reply. Instead, some months later, after Marie had recovered from her illness, an officer of the Royal Guards suddenly appeared at the remote country estate of Mme de Chevreuse with an order for her to proceed to Angoulême. The officer was charged with conducting her there at once.

The castle of Angoulême was a place used for the strictest confinement; it was there that Châteauneuf had suffered his ten years of imprisonment. To be deported there meant the end, and Marie knew she would never come out again. On the other hand this sudden decision to get rid of her after one and a half years of banishment was a sign that the fear of her and of her influence was still very much alive, as well as proof of the rising discontent in the country. And so, with a smiling face and in the friendliest manner, she told the officer that she would naturally obey the order of the Queen and travel with him to Angoulême. But as an officer of the Royal Guard he would certainly understand that she and her daughter must choose and gather the clothes and belongings which they would need there, and that it might take a couple of hours until everything was ready and packed. She hoped, therefore, that as a nobleman he would be prepared to wait that long and in the meantime would accept some refreshments.

The officer, who had expected painful scenes and resistance, was agreeably surprised and understandingly prepared to wait patiently until the ladies were ready. He enjoyed the meal that was served to him, and then waited and waited, and, when he finally felt that too much time had passed, he went through the rambling house in search of the ladies, to hurry them up. But they were nowhere to be found. They had disappeared.

Without losing a moment, and taking only her jewels and the money that was ready to hand, Marie had left the house by a side door and had driven off with her daughter in one of her coaches accompanied by two servants. She had already been gone for some hours and nobody knew which route she had taken. A coach with two ladies and two servants would not seem at all conspicuous.

This time, her flight was not as adventurous as had been her escape eight years earlier. She drove straight to Brittany where, as she knew, dissatisfaction was rampant because of various measures that interfered with the ancient customs of the province. Then she crossed Brittany towards St Malo and stopped her coach outside the town at the castle of the Governor, the Marquis de Coatquin, an old friend of the Rohans. When she pleaded for the means with which to travel to England, he proved to be a true Breton and worthy of her trust. He immediately sent a servant to the harbour, who discovered that there was an English boat preparing to sail for Dartmouth. The skipper was willing to take passengers, and Marie embarked with her daughter after taking the precaution of leaving her jewels in the custody of her friend. The ship sailed, and after its departure the Marquis de Coatquin wrote a letter to Mazarin, informing him that Mme de Chevreuse had left for England.

As Marie was in any case outside his jurisdiction, Mazarin preferred not to make another enemy among the powerful nobles of that restive province and thanked him ironically for the information: 'I have, as you desired, taken your attitude in this matter as proof of the faithful performance of your duty to the Government.' But he did not fail to add that he had reported the matter to the Queen.

If Marie now believed she would be able to travel in freedom and security through England to Dunkirk and from there to Liège, from where she intended to start fresh negotiations with Anne, all her hopes were very soon shattered. Scarcely was the boat in sight of the English coast when two warships carrying the Parliamentary flag intercepted it. The boat was searched and the captains recognized Mme de Chevreuse. They knew her to be a friend of the royal family, and the Queen of England, they knew, was in France, while Charles I was now desperately seeking help from abroad. Could she not be the bearer of some important message for him? The captains of the warships declared that they could not allow her to land in England. They would convey her to the Isle of Wight, where she would have to await the decision of Parliament.

Thus Marie and her daughter were landed on the Isle of Wight. There she learned that the Governor of the island was the Earl of Pembroke whom she knew from her previous sojourns in England; but he was in London, so she wrote to him that she had been forced to leave France to escape persecution by her enemies and was seeking refuge in a neutral country. 'As the power of my enemies sought to rob me totally of my freedom, the only way I could find to escape this injustice was to flee from St Malo to England. From there I shall travel to Liège, where I definitely hope to be able to prove that I am guiltless.' She begged him to get from Parliament permission for her to travel to Dover and there to embark for Dunkirk, where she would be able to put her affairs in order.

Pembroke appealed on her behalf to Parliament, but it refused to set her free or to allow her to travel through England. Parliament even made an offer to Mazarin to hand her over, but Mazarin declined with thanks. He was happy to know that she was detained by the English on the Isle of Wight, cut off from any contact. He had no valid case against her to put before a court, as she had not committed any offence which could be proved in law. Even if his spies had intercepted some of her letters to her friends in Flanders, she could declare in court that she had only been following the example of the Queen, who had done the same under Richelieu, and that would create a tremendous stir. And to keep her imprisoned without a proper sentence would mean setting more noble families against him. As when Richelieu had been satisfied that she was stranded hopeless in Dunkirk, so Mazarin was still more content to know that she was cut off from everybody in the isolation of the Isle of Wight.

Marie was desperate. She fell ill again. Her money had gone and she wrote to the Marquis de Coatquin, asking him to hand over the jewels she had left with him to a friend in Paris, Montrésor, to whom she sent a special messenger to bring them to her, because she was without other means of subsistence. Mazarin heard of this transaction, and while he had reacted to the information about her flight with only an ironical letter, at the news that Montrésor had handed over Marie's jewels to her agent, he immediately arrested and imprisoned him. It was said that Mazarin, now busily amassing riches for himself, wanted to appropriate the famous jewellery that had originated with Concini and Luynes. Montrésor had to suffer more than a year's imprisonment in Vincennes until the intervention of the Guise family secured his release.

In the meantime Marie, after waiting for three long months on the Isle of Wight, succeeded in establishing contact with the Spanish Ambassador in London, who applied to Parliament on her behalf; and as Charles I had just been decisively defeated in the battle of Naseby, Parliament gave her permission to travel to Dover and there to embark for Dunkirk. From Dunkirk she went with her daughter to Brussels and then to Liège.

But her hope of reaching some kind of understanding with Anne was dashed. The situation in Paris was described by a contemporary as follows:

'The stairs of the Palais Royal are just as slippery as those of the Louvre ever were: this is a queer country, in which honest people can achieve very little. Monsieur Mazarin is an absolute ruler: and all others tremble or bow low before the glory of the Cardinal!'

Marie tried to get her husband to plead for her, but the Duc de Chevreuse was afraid for his own position at Court. All he could say to Mazarin was that he himself condemned his wife's intrigues. Meanwhile, Mazarin spared neither money nor efforts to keep Marie, now in Flanders, under strict observation and received almost daily reports about her activities.

Although she could no longer pretend to have any influence at the French Court, she was welcomed by all her old friends and, recognizing that she had nothing to hope for from the present Government, she quickly established contact with all the Cardinal's opponents. He believed he could feel her hand everywhere. Was it just a coincidence that the Duc de Beaufort suddenly managed to escape from Vincennes and reached the papal enclave of Avignon? Was it a coincidence that Anne was being urged again from all sides to make an end of the war against Spain – by the nuns of Val-de-Grâce and all the high clerics in touch with her, by the English Queen Henriette-Marie, and even by the Condé family? The old Condé had died and d'Enghien, having become the head of the family and having inherited the title, seemed no longer interested in continuing the war; there were even rumours in circulation of an impending private understanding between Condé and the Spaniards, of preparation for a new rising of the Huguenots, as well as of the doubtful loyalty of some army commanders.

Mazarin spread the idea abroad that all this was the result of Marie's activity; but, in fact, conditions within France had been gradually worsening. The Government itself suffered from an acute lack of money. While the Court outwardly maintained an appearance of luxury and Mazarin himself was amassing a private fortune, there was not money enough in the treasury even to pay the troops. Many foreign mercenaries abandoned the army and returned home. They were replaced by vagabonds and beggars who had been seized in the streets. Officers on leave failed to return to their regiments, and Mazarin ordered their arrest and sent them under escort back to the war. If some successes were still achieved, they were matched by defeats in other engagements.

Mazarin had a new controller of finance, an Italian, who, in search of fresh sources of taxation, found an old edict prohibiting all building in the belt of land outside the walls of Paris; nearly the whole area was now built up, and so he demanded a tax on every square yard of every building. This resulted in a rising which could only be suppressed by the use of force. The owners of these houses appealed to Parlement, and Parlement, in spite of Anne's contemptuous rebuff, refused to register the order necessary to make these demands lawful. Mazarin saw himself forced to abandon this tax for the time being; but the need for money grew, and soon there was no longer any question of keeping the state of finances secret. As the Venetian envoy reported: 'The administration of the State is in such disorder that His Majesty [the eight-year-old Louis XIV] never has a sou of ready cash. As the treasury is exhausted, they make appropriations in advance on the funds due to come in, and draw on next year's revenue.'

As taxes were mortgaged, the tax-collectors ruthlessly enforced the payment of the tax-debts, and often fraudulently. The peasantry was ruined, the land remained uncultivated, and Marie recognized that it was only a matter of time before disturbances would break out. She did not cease to warn her Spanish friends of this. And when those disturbances finally came, they assumed such proportions that the whole structure of the State was shaken.

Chapter IX

'For ten years the countryside has been bankrupt. The peasants have been reduced to sleeping on straw, their furniture having been sold to pay the taxes which they could not meet, and millions of innocent human beings are forced to live on tears and coarse bread in order to pamper the fearful and rampant luxury of the capital. They own nothing but their souls, because souls cannot be sold by auction. Now, after paying for the food and winter-quarters of Your Majesty's troops, after discharging market tolls and loans as well as the royal and manorial dues, the inhabitants of the towns are to be asked to pay further taxes . . .'

That was the reply given by Omer Talon, the Attorney-General, when on January 15, 1648, Anne, with the nine-year-old Louis, held a *lit de justice* in the Parlement of Paris, demanding the registration of new financial edicts imposing further heavy burdens upon the people.

At the solemn meeting of the *lit de justice*, Parlemnt had the 'right of remonstrance', which meant that it could express its doubts about the measures proposed and bring its objections before the King, although afterwards it was its duty to register the demands, whether altered or not, so that these would become law. Omer Talon now addressed himself directly to the Queen:

'Be pleased, Madame, to reflect in the depths of your heart on these public misfortunes. Think of the sorrows of your people, who cannot be nourished by the honours of battles won and cities captured, who are without bread, for myrtles, palms and laurels are not reckoned among the ordinary fruits of the earth. . .'

However, the Paris Parlement was no more than a judicial body, consisting mainly of lawyers who had inherited or purchased their posts and whose primary function was to try the more important civil and criminal cases. Not many years earlier it had been commanded by Louis XIII to 'register and publish his ordinances and edicts without any discussion'; afterwards its members had been told by Richelieu 'that they were to obey without further argument, as it was the duty of the Parlement to make the King's orders into laws by registering them'. Therefore, these new burdens were also duly registered. But Parlement took an unprecedented step: together with the delegates of the three other highest sovereign courts, the Board of Excise, the Grand Council and the Court of Accounts, it elected a special committee to examine these edicts and to discuss reforms.

Anne demanded that these discussions should cease forthwith, but the delegates continued to meet and to confer. They formed a chamber, called after their meeting place 'the Chamber of St Louis', refusing to let their freedom of deliberation be curtailed by this 'foreign woman and her Italian Machiavelli'. Finally, the Chamber produced a long list of demands for the abolition of 'abuses which had crept into the State administration', for the reduction of various taxes, for a reform of the finance department and above all for a guarantee of personal liberty, so that nobody could any longer be arrested and imprisoned without a court sentence. Anne fumed: such claims were sheer impudence, an encroachment on the power of the crown; but Mazarin explained to her that in the present situation the Government had no alternative but to negotiate quietly without inflaming feelings further, since it had no money and no new loans were available. Every purse was closed and if the troops remained unpaid the army would disband. Anne herself had already been forced to borrow cash from the Princesse de Condé to pay the Swiss Guards of her own Court.

Under such conditions Anne was obliged to sanction the joint meetings of 'the Chamber of St Louis', and Mazarin began to negotiate with the delegates. He seemed to be prepared to compromise: he discharged the hated Controller of Finances, agreed to reduce some of the taxes and to recall some of the 'Intendants' – Government agents first established in the provinces by Richelieu, who exercised the real power there while the nobles appointed as governors were being reduced to figureheads, deriving only honour and income from their appointments. Finally he even promised that any new financial measures would first be submitted to Parlement for examination. Thus, in spite of a hint that in future Parlement must confine itself to its judicial functions, it was fully aware that it had won the contest, and at the next *lit de justice* on July 31st, called to register the amended edicts replacing the revoked ones, Omer Talon declared:

'The control which was formerly exercised by the nobility of the realm has now devolved upon Parlement, whose voice is the expression of the will of the people. Therefore the protests occasionally made by the magistrates should, instead of being interpreted as a sign of disobedience, be regarded as one of the duties of their office.'

Neither Anne nor Mazarin really intended to accept this control by the rebellious *noblesse de robe*, as these representatives of the middle class, whom the garment of office had ennobled, were called. However, these rebels were soon known as 'Frondeurs', at first derisively; the name was a derivation from the word *fronde*, a sling used by street urchins for throwing stones before they ran away at the approach of the city guards. Anne and Mazarin only awaited the right opportunity to use the Guards against the rebels and they felt that the time had come when, after some military failures, Condé won an important victory over the Spaniards at Lens. Mazarin called out enthusiastically, 'Heaven has at last declared itself in our favour, in Flanders not less than in other fields,' and the State Council decided that this was the appropriate occasion to take revenge for the presumption of Parlement.

A thanksgiving service in the Cathedral of Notre Dame was arranged. The whole route of the royal procession was lined with troops, giving an impressive display of the armed forces still maintained in the capital by the Government which should intimidate any opposition.

Anne ordered the immediate arrest of the three most outspoken members of Parlement, and to demonstrate that the Government would tolerate no insubordination the arrests were to be made in full daylight. One of the three was not at home; the other two were arrested, and, when the most popular of them was being led away, his servant-maid tore open a window and shouted into the street that he had been seized with violence. The populace of Paris rose at once. Everyone rushed to arms, and barricades appeared in the streets to the very precincts of the Palais Royal. Paul Gondi, the Coadjutor, and nephew of the Archbishop of Paris, whose fiery speeches had made him a favourite with the crowds, rushed in his robes to the Palace, asked for an audience and offered to restore order if the arrested men were released. Anne refused and ordered the troops to disperse the crowds. A hail of stones met the soldiers; shooting started and lasted throughout the night. Next morning Parlement assembled and sent a delegation to the Regent to beg for the release of the arrested. Anne rejected the demand in spite of the warning of the First President of Parlement, Molé, 'that it would be wiser to grant with good grace what in the end must inevitably be yielded to force'.

The delegates themselves, when they were seen returning without the prisoners, who were thought to be held in the vicinity of the Palace, had to run a gauntlet of insults and curses and were menaced with violence. Mazarin, preparing to flee at a moment's notice if the situation became too dangerous, persuaded Anne to sign the order for the release of the arrested, who had already been taken away from Paris. The promise was not believed and the riots continued throughout the day and the night until the following morning, when the arrested councillors got back to the capital.

Now Parlement gave the order that the barricades should be demolished and everyone should lay down their arms. The shops reopened, and soon everything was quiet and orderly. But towards the evening two heavily laden carts, escorted by some guards, were seen leaving the arsenal. They were immediately surrounded and it was found that they contained bullets and barrels of gunpowder. They were looted; rumours were spread that the Queen wanted to fire on the people, and the barricades rose again. All windows were lit, in case the royal troops might make a surprise attack by night.

Mazarin wrote in his diary:

'The affront to the King by Parlement and a section of the people of Paris could not have been worse either in form or in manner and it was displayed so ostentatiously that there is not a corner in France or even in Europe that has not heard of it and that is not waiting to see the outcome of it. . . . The rebels have acted in a public and unprecedented manner, and Parlement, far from denouncing them, has shown by its behaviour that it approves all they have done. . . . Parlement has assumed the functions of the King and the people have entirely acquiesced in this. . . .

141

They have spoken contemptuously of the Queen and of myself. They have made insolent and outrageous proposals to expel me and to place the Regent in a convent. . . .'

Both Anne and Mazarin were longing for revenge. The rebels should be taught a lesson. An urgent call for Condé went out, and then, less than three weeks after the day of the barricades, the royal family with Gaston, Mazarin and other members of the government moved off by night to Rueil. When Condé arrived there in all haste, it was decided in the Queen's Council that he should draw all available troops to Paris, besiege the capital and enforce the Government's rule. In the meantime Mazarin would continue the negotiations with the more moderate councillors who had obeyed his order to come to Rueil.

These negotiations led to a new compromise, securing and confirming the rights and privileges of Parlement and regulating the financial, judicial and commercial administration, and Anne even signed an ordinance which promised the abolition of arbitrary arrest and imprisonment without trial. Thereupon a delegation headed by the Mayor of Paris came to Rueil begging for the return of the Court, because its absence, with the houses of the princes and the great nobles shut, was damaging to commerce. So six weeks after its flight the Government returned to the capital and was welcomed with the usual rejoicing.

Again, Mazarin did not for a moment consider carrying out his promises despite the complaints of Parlement; its President declared that 'the State had become a prey to grave disorders through the misgovernment of the King's ministers, and to cure these evils it was necessary to strike at their root'. Thus all attacks now concentrated on Mazarin and a wave of defamatory pamphlets – called Mazarinades – appeared. Libellous posters were stuck up everywhere and the Parisians gathered in front of each one, enjoying the satirical abuse of the Minister, and also of the Queen.

In the meantime the news spread that Condé's troops were making their way towards Paris, and the leaders of the discontented, who now, with the attacks concentrated on Mazarin, included many high nobles, held meetings to decide what steps should be taken. The best remedy would be increased activity by the Spanish in Flanders, which would force Condé to keep his soldiers there, and the Coadjutor Gondi, who became increasingly the outspoken leader of the Frondeurs, decided that an approach to Mme de Chevreuse would be most useful. The envoy selected was the 35-year-old Marquis de Laigue, who had previously been an officer in Condé's army, but offended by the Prince's arrogant behaviour had left the military service, moved to Paris and joined the Fronde.

From Flanders, Marie had carefully observed the events in Paris, for they were what she had long prophesied. Even the participation of Parlement did not surprise her, for already, before her flight to England, one of her trusted friends had sounded out the feelings of the Chamber against Mazarin, and the fact that Parlement had now openly joined the fight against the Government meant that it foresaw the possibility of victory. After the arrival of de Laigue in Brussels, she approached the Archduke Leopold, but as the winter was on its way there could be no question of an immediate Spanish offensive and Condé could therefore continue with the withdrawal of his troops, while in the meantime he and Gaston assured Parlement that all the undertakings given would be fulfilled.

While the troops were approaching Paris, before any action could be undertaken, it was naturally necessary to conduct the royal family to safety, and again in the middle of the night Anne, with Louis, Mazarin and their closest adherents, as well as Gaston and Condé, fled to St Germain. St Germain was only a summer residence and the flight took place on January 5, 1649. The palace was, therefore, stripped of all furniture for the winter; there were no beds, no blankets. The courtiers, the dukes, duchesses and ministers were fortunate if they could gather some straw to lie on; otherwise they had to sleep on bare floors in ice-cold rooms.

Next day the Parisians received, together with the news of the Court's flight, a proclamation from the Queen that she and Louis had had to seek safety because of the 'arbitrary and criminal intentions and dealings of the gentlemen of Parlement'. Parlement countered with an enactment pronouncing Mazarin 'a disturber of the peace, an enemy of the King and of the State' with a demand for his dismissal. In the Town Hall a kind of provisional government was formed, and Parlement instructed this city government to organize the defence and the provisioning of Paris. As the people espied carts carrying furniture and other commodities through the streets they prevented these from leaving and looted them. All the gates of the city were closed and the civil guards were doubled.

The task of organizing the defence forces was entrusted to Gondi, who enjoyed the confidence of the populace, and he called the people to arms and reinforced the city walls; every nobleman who wanted to join the rebels was enthusiastically received and given some commanding position, since only the nobles had any knowledge of military matters, the army being their only socially acceptable profession. The Parisians were astonished to see how many of them were joining the resistance movement; not only those who had been banned from Court, like the Duc de Beaufort or the Duc de Bouillon, who was still deprived of his Sedan, but even the Prince de Conti, Condé's own brother, and his brother-in-law, the Duc de Longueville, left St Germain and came to Paris to accept a command there. As the rising was officially directed only against Mazarin, most of the nobles in Paris felt themselves in sympathy with the rebels. Even the 72-year-old Duc de Chevreuse joined them and was seen high on his horse among the militia. When he later approached Anne to appeal for permission for Marie to return to France and she mocked him about his feelings for the Fronde, his only excuse was: 'I, too, am a Parisian.'

Anne wanted Condé to attack Paris, but he declared he had not enough troops to take the capital. All he could do was to occupy the strategic points in the suburbs and surroundings to prevent boats with grain, flour and other provisions from entering, thus cutting off the food supplies. Within the town the improvised militia had taken the arsenal and, after a few cannon shots, the Bastille too, but they were beaten back when they tried to face Condé's troops in a sortie and forced to retreat into the town. Famine was threatening, and Parlement decided to send a delegation to St Germain, particularly as, after the pressure from Mme de Chevreuse, an envoy from the Archduke Leopold had arrived with a letter to Parlement proposing negotiations to end the war.

That was intended to give the Parisians convincing evidence that Spain wanted peace, and if the hostilities were to continue this would prove to be the fault of no one but Mazarin. The appearance of the envoy led to a stormy debate in Parlement, exposing the strong antagonism between the majority of the councillors and the noisy but smaller group of radicals who, together with the rebellious nobles, dominated the populace. The majority of Parlement was afraid to start negotiations with the Archduke on their own responsibility and decided to inform the Queen. Although the Court lived in St Germain in wretched conditions, for no money was coming in and Condé's unpaid troops maintained themselves by pillaging the occupied suburbs, Anne received the delegation with very little graciousness and demanded the complete submission of Parlement.

Mazarin and Condé understood the position better; they negotiated, but the conditions they proposed were so harsh and humiliating that at the meeting of Parlement which was to ratify them the mob stormed the building and the delegates had to flee for their lives. Next day, when tempers had cooled a bit, Parlement decided to send another delegation demanding amendments and in particular a clause protecting the nobles who had joined their cause from any persecution. Various nobles whose possessions in the country had been damaged or looted demanded compensation and made special requests, and the Prince de Conti, as well as Marie's son, the Duc de Luynes, whose castle at Lésigny had been looted and burnt, included in their list of requests permission for Mme de Chevreuse 'to return to France and live in safety and freedom at Court or wherever she wanted'.

This time Mazarin proved amenable. The Archduke had actually started a new military campaign in Flanders; from England had come the news of the execution of King Charles; and if the hungry and rebellious Paris mob were now to destroy Parlement, Mazarin would be faced with chaos. He told Anne that conditions in France could become like those in England where the civil war had led to the downfall of the monarchy. He had heard that Marshal Turenne, in command of the army in Germany, wanted to come to the aid of Paris. So Mazarin collected all the money available and sent it to Turenne's foreign mercenaries on condition that they left the army; in this way Turenne's advance was stopped. Other discontented nobles were even raising troops in the provinces. An agreement acceptable to all factions of Parlement had to be reached, and thus a full pardon to all rebels was conceded, food was allowed into Paris, and even everyone's safety from arrest and imprisonment without trial was confirmed. On their part, the Frondeurs promised the disbandment of the militia.

K

This treaty of Rueil was ratified on April 1, 1649, and although it gave to all exiles the right of return, tradition demanded that Mme de Chevreuse should wait for a summons from the Queen. She waited a week, she waited ten days, but nothing came. She had sent de Laigue, who had become her lover, in advance and he reached Paris without any trouble. When she heard from her friends that every time they asked Anne to include her name in the list of people 'welcomed, so that she might go anywhere and live in any part of the kingdom', the Queen's reaction had been a sarcastic smile. So Marie suddenly left Brussels with her daughter Charlotte and travelled from Cambrai without stopping at any place before reaching Paris.

On her arrival on April 12th she found a pamphlet being sold everywhere in the streets with the title *The French Amazon or the Help for the Parisians represented by the Illustrious Conqueror*. It ecstatically praised her heroic virtues, described her constancy and her valorous deeds and ended with the claim that she was 'the hope of our peace who has come to our help against oppression by monsters; a sun that appears to rise in order to drive away the mists of misfortune that pile up over our heads; an enchanting Aurora full of the luminous rays of righteous wrath at the dawn of our most hopeful day'. The welcome accorded to her by her friends and the leaders of the Fronde, who came rushing to the Hôtel de Chevreuse to greet the famous fugitive, was equally enthusiastic; but from the Government, in the name of the Queen, she received an instruction to go within twenty-four hours to Dampierre for a month's retirement, after which time she could apply for the Queen's permission to come to Paris.

She immediately drove to the First President of Parlement, Mathieu Molé, the man who had arranged the treaty, but his remonstrances only brought the answer that this was an order which Mme de Chevreuse had to obey, otherwise the Government would have to bring her to her senses. Marie sent de Laigue to Gondi; Gondi also went to Molé, who in the meantime had applied to Mazarin, stressing the popularity which Mme de Chevreuse enjoyed among the people and advising him not to go too far in this matter. Mazarin cancelled the order. Marie was for the time being able to remain in Paris; but Anne could not endure the thought that Marie had defied her, so after a few days she renewed the request that she should retire for some period of time to Dampierre. Marie wrote to Mazarin and long negotiations began, with Molé as mediator.

Marie declared that she was prepared to show her obedience to the Queen, but she wanted precise information about how long her retirement would last and demanded assurance for her safe return. Mazarin warned Anne not to create any further difficulties over Mme de Chevreuse; he had troubles enough. Besides, it might be possible to win Marie's collaboration which would be very useful in the present circumstances. Nevertheless, the negotiations lasted so long that it was nearly mid-July before Marie left for Dampierre and after a few days petitioned for permission to pay her respects to Her Majesty, which meant to be accepted again in full favour. Anne at once gave her consent and, as custom demanded, a courtier was sent to Dampierre to escort the Duchess to Compiègne, where the Court was spending the summer. However, Marie fell ill, and two weeks elapsed before she could present herself at Court.

When she arrived, now in her late forties, pale and worn out by the illness, and begged, as required, the Queen's pardon for all her past actions, promising unshakable loyalty in future, Anne did not make any reproaches. She let her greet the young Louis, now approaching his eleventh year, and then exchange a few words with Mazarin. But scarcely had she left the room when the Queen loudly remarked, so that everybody could hear her, that Mme de Chevreuse no longer retained any trace of her former beauty. In contrast, everyone present admired the dazzling beauty of her now 23-year-old daughter Charlotte.

In any case, after this reception it seemed that Marie had succeeded in re-establishing herself at the Court. The Court *Gazette* carried reports of her accompanying the Queen with other great ladies to a special church service, and that, at the celebration of the eleventh birthday of Louis, the little King had danced with Gaston's daughter while the Prince de Condé had partnered Mlle de Chevreuse. However, this apparent harmony was just as deceptive as the show of happiness at Court. The man most affected by Charlotte's charm was the 35-year-old Coadjutor Gondi. He fell deeply in love with the girl who, he maintained, had 'the most beautiful eyes in the world and her own particular way of using them', and Marie did not discourage the love affair because, so long as it lasted, she held Gondi in her hands and could with his help maintain her influence over all the divergent forces of the Fronde. The Government's renewed feeling of disquiet was not at all in keeping with the festive atmosphere deliberately displayed at Court. 'Mazarinades' were constantly appearing now and the more offensive they were the greater the populace enjoyed them. Moreover, Mazarin now felt that his own position was menaced from within the Court itself.

He had continually warned Anne not to put too much trust in Condé because 'if he prevails, he will in the end hold Your government, Your person and the King at his mercy. The surrender of Paris will make Condé the dictator of this realm until Louis reaches the age of maturity. In the meantime what will Your own fate be? And what will be mine?' Now, since Paris had surrendered and Condé felt himself to be the saviour of the monarchy, he also wanted to be its arbiter. He not only claimed positions of power and government for his relatives and friends, but he strove to reduce Mazarin to a mere cipher. Already while the Court was still at Compiègne he had gone to Parlement in Paris. He was enthusiastically received and given an address of welcome, as both parties thought that they could win him to their side. When he returned to Compiègne he contradicted every idea put forward by Mazarin, demanded to be consulted on every act of patronage, and when Anne supported Mazarin he simply walked out of the Council.

As the Archduke Leopold's offensive continued, with the loss of several towns, Mazarin offered Condé the position of Supreme Commander in Flanders, which he had previously desired; but this time the Prince declined. It was not in his interest to go away at present. As Parlement had refused to discuss the urgent financial measures so long as the Government was away, the Court returned to Paris after seven months of absence, but here Condé's attitude to Mazarin became still more hostile. He declared publicly that he had upheld Mazarin because he had pledged his word to do so, but if matters took a different course he would consider himself at perfect liberty to withdraw his protection from the Minister. His natural pride and insolence had been enormously increased by the events of the last few months; he seemed to see in every action of Mazarin a carefully calculated move to strengthen the Cardinal's position or to lower his own prestige. His demands for strategic positions for his relatives were increasing, and when Mazarin would not agree he shook his fist in the Cardinal's face and left the room.

Mazarin tried to win the support of the other princes of royal blood, the Vendômes, who were the enemies of the Condés. One of the sons of the Duc de Vendôme intended to marry one of Mazarin's nieces, while another niece was to become engaged to a son of the Duc d'Epernon, who ruled over Guyenne, which had previously belonged to the Condés. But recognizing that the connection with the Vendômes would strengthen the Cardinal's position, Condé warned Mazarin not to proceed with these marriages, otherwise he would go to Parlement and demand that the law, passed under Luynes after Concini's assassination, which forbade any foreigner to act as Minister, would be brought into action. Under this threat Mazarin was forced to yield and even to promise 'not to accord any regencies, high positions or to send any envoys, nor ban any persons from Court or make decisions of importance without consulting the Prince in advance'. In return Condé consented to a reconciliation and promised to 'restore by all possible means the authority of the King as it was previously and to act in the interests of the Cardinal and the State as he would in his own against all persons, whomsoever they were'.

This agreement bound Mazarin completely; on the other hand, it also destroyed every hope of the Fronde to get rid of the Cardinal with Condé's help and to establish a government agreeable to them. The arrogant remark by the Prince that Parlement was a gang of bourgeois 'impudently aiming at governing the State', changed the attitude of the men who had welcomed him so warmly at his first visit. The Hôtel de Chevreuse became the centre where all the phases of the struggle between Condé and Mazarin were observed and commented upon and where the changing feelings of Parlement were discussed. It was about two months after the Court's return to Paris that Mme de Chevreuse decided to take action. At one of her visits to the Palais Royal she engaged Mazarin in a private conversation and declared to him that the only way to re-establish the authority of the Government was to arrest Condé.

Mazarin did not even dare to consider the possibility of such a step. What would be the reaction of Parlement, of the Fronde, of the populace? And, as Condé was the supreme leader, how would the army react? But Marie knew the right answer to every question. Parlement was disillusioned. As regards the attitude of the Fronde, that was Mazarin's own fault. Instead of being an enemy of the Frondeurs he should become their protector; then all their leaders would be prepared to support the Government, and with their hold over the populace they would see to it that there were no disturbances. Although Condé was generalissimo, Gaston's rank was higher still and she could obtain Gaston's agreement. If Condé was allowed to carry on as he was, he would soon be the commander of everybody and everything, but 'the Prince was not what he was believed to be; he was only strong among the weak, but very weak among the strong'.

Mazarin was overwhelmed by the idea, but much too frightened to risk such a venture, and Marie had to have several meetings with him to make him think at all of the feasibility of this step. To get a decision she also approached Anne and stressed the difficulties of the Regency when a prince such as Condé considered himself above the Government. But in fact it was a quite different instance of Condé's insolence which very soon forced the Queen to follow Marie's recommendation.

Condé intended to gain control of the fortress of Le Havre which was nominally under the governorship of Richelieu's young nephew. Being still less than twenty years old, this young Duc de Richelieu was under the guardianship of his aunt, the Duchesse d'Aiguillon, who was in the process of arranging a marriage between him and Marie's daughter Charlotte. The young Duke himself had started a flirtation with a thirty-year-old widow, Mme de Pons, and had fallen in love with her. Thereupon Condé invited the pair to his country house near Paris, and arranged for his chaplain to marry them an hour after their arrival, he himself giving away the bride. As he wanted the young Richelieu to hold Le Havre for him, he sent the newly married couple back home immediately, fully expecting that, as soon as the news reached Court, the Queen would issue orders that entry into the citadel should be forbidden to them.

The Duchesse d'Aiguillon despatched a desperate letter to Anne, so that when Condé insolently came to see the Queen she told him that the offended Duchess would obtain a decree annulling the marriage of a minor. But his haughty answer was: 'Not when a person of my rank has signed as a witness.'

Marie was enraged at the insult inflicted on herself and on her daughter, and when she arrived at the Palais Royal and found the Queen furious and Mazarin full of bitter resentment, she did not miss the opportunity to insist that the arrest of Condé was the only way to ensure tranquillity in the country. If the Queen needed help she could have it from the Fronde, whose leaders were her loyal subjects. To Anne's reply that enemies of Mazarin could scarcely by loyal, she gave her prepared answer that, if the Cardinal would agree to become the patron of the Frondeurs, they would be delighted to be his friends and allies.

The result of this meeting was a note from Anne inviting Gondi to a secret private audience of which nobody except Mme and Mlle de Chevreuse should know – an assurance made to him in case his own followers became suspicious. The audience took place at midnight in the Queen's prayer room, to which he was led by her attendant. Anne was full of lamentations about Condé, Mazarin added his own complaints, and Gondi assured her of his allegiance. As a sequel to this audience various meetings with Mazarin followed to which Mme de Chevreuse brought other leaders of the Fronde and even her friend and lover de Laigue, who was to become Captain of the Guards to Louis's younger brother.

She soon won over Gaston, too, who was already jealous of Condé's increasing influence, and when Marie demonstrated to him that the Prince's claim to have the right to decide every appointment and promotion was an infringement of rights attached to his own position as Lieutenant-General of the Realm, and that with Condé's disappearance he, Gaston, would become the most influential figure in France, he gave his consent to the arrest, though, always loath to commit himself openly, he naturally abstained from taking any part in the meetings. It was January before agreement about all the proposed appointments and nominations was reached.

For some time news of unusual movements among the troops belonging to Condé, his brother Conti, and his brother-in-law, the Duc de Longueville, had been circulating, so that Mazarin made this note: 'I am told that the Prince has sent for a large number of the lesser nobility in his governorship and for officers of his troops.

Those in his household who are most in his confidence say that he is hatching some big plot.' He promised Gondi the desired Cardinal's hat and no longer resisted Marie's demand for the Great Seal to be passed to Châteauneuf, who was now seventy years of age.

As soon as the agreement on all points was reached, Anne called an urgent meeting of the State Council for January 18th. When the members of the Government began to arrive, they heard that the Queen was ill; Gaston had sent an excuse that he could not attend; Mazarin was not yet present; and when the Princes Condé and Conti, with the Duc de Longueville, arrived, the commander of the Guards entered the room with two lieutenants and declared the three princes under arrest in the name of the Queen. Then he led them through a secret passage to a coach with drawn blinds and escorted them with a squadron of light horse to Vincennes. The arrest was accomplished so quietly that the princes' attendants were still waiting in the courtyard long afterwards, until finally they were informed. Then they rushed to Condé's palace to discuss what counter-stroke could be undertaken.

During this time the Hôtel de Chevreuse was also busy. Mme de Chevreuse was considering what action should follow the arrest, and decided that Gondi should issue an ordinance to all Paris priests instructing them how to communicate the news from their parish pulpits. Afterwards, all those present drove to the Palais du Luxembourg to pay a ceremonial visit to Gaston, whom they found nervously whistling and pacing up and down the room with his hands in his pockets.

In Condé's palace his partisans were assembling. Eventually, they decided to storm the convent of Val-de-Grâce and take Mazarin's nieces as hostages. But when they arrived at the convent they were informed by the nuns that the girls were no longer there; some hours earlier they had been taken to the Palais Royal. Then Condé's followers observed that all the streets were swarming with people cheering the news of the arrests, and as it grew dark bonfires were lit and the Parisians began to sing and to dance. This demonstration showed how unpopular Condé's behaviour had made him, and so his partisans now preferred to leave Paris and to hurry to their provinces.

In the Palais Royal the day finished with a great reception for the gentlemen of the Fronde, and the salons were thronged with nobles who had come to offer their services to the Queen and Mazarin. Next day, an address from the Queen reached Parlement with a long description of Condé's 'insolent defiance of the authority of the throne and the respect due to it', which had forced her to consign the princes to Vincennes. She justified the arbitrary arrests because, 'as the governors of Burgundy, Champagne, Normandy, Bresse and Berry, they had power over navigation on all the great rivers of the realm', which meant that they were able to cut Paris off from its supplies of food. This explanation was received with deference, and, remembering the recent food shortage in the capital, Parlement voted for sending a humble address to the Queen approving her action.

Now Anne felt herself in full control; the Frondeurs had become her new allies and were eager to serve her. All she had to do was to go into the provinces, where Condé's followers were collecting their forces, and 'to pursue and crush her enemies'. But before her departure she sent for the Duc de Mercoeur, a son of Vendôme, and had his betrothal with Mazarin's niece celebrated in her presence.

Marie, on her part, was at the peak of her power. She had not only succeeded in re-establishing her position, but was recognized by all parties and she had influence everywhere. Anne seemed to have lost her aversion to Mme de Chevreuse's intrusions into the affairs of State and once more treated her as an old and devoted friend. The Frondeurs did not fail to recognize that they owed their new position to her, while they all naturally continued to work eagerly for their own utmost advantage by gaining the ear of Gaston or Mazarin. And Mazarin played before Mme de Chevreuse the role of devoted and sincere friend, sent her his highest officials to enquire her opinion on any matters arising, and acted according to her advice. Nevertheless it was not long before she discovered that all his assurances and promises were to be kept only so long as it suited him.

Chapter X

On the day of the princes' arrest, Anne sent a courtier to Condé's sister, the Duchesse de Longueville, who, like Mme de Chevreuse, was deeply involved in the politics of the time, inviting her to come to the Palais Royal. The Duchess was not at home, and when the news of the arrests spread she immediately went into hiding. A few days later she managed to escape from Paris, fled to Normandy, which had been under her husband's rule, and began to incite the province to revolt. Thus Anne's first move was to go with Mazarin and all available troops to Normandy, where she found that the townspeople did not want a civil war in the least, so that when the royal troops approached the gates of the cities and fortresses were opened without resistance, and the Duchess had to flee once more. She tried to find refuge in Le Havre, but the young Richelieu, under the influence of his wife, who regarded the possession of the fortress as more important than gratitude to Condé for arranging their marriage, closed the gates to the Duchess and advised her to return to Paris and submit to the Queen, while he himself, together with other Norman dignitaries, answered Anne's call and came to renew their oaths of loyalty and obedience. After a campaign of no more than three weeks, the Court was able to return to Paris.

Marie immediately made use of the Court's return to bring Châteauneuf into the Palais Royal, where the Queen accorded him a gracious reception and personally presented him with the Great Seal. Mazarin, who had so long prevented the inclusion of Châteauneuf in the State Council, could do nothing but congratulate him on his reinstatement. The period of rest in Paris, however, was to last only a few days, as the campaign against Condé's associates in other provinces had to be pursued. During the Queen's and her Minister's absence, power in the capital naturally lay in the hands of Gaston, whom Mazarin did not trust; therefore he ordered his most devoted officials in Paris to keep him continually informed of every decision and every step taken.

The attitude of the people in Burgundy and adjoining territories proved to be the same as in Normandy. All towns opened their gates, welcomed the Queen and particularly greeted the boy-king Louis, whom Anne and Mazarin did not dare to leave in Paris during their absence. Every personage summoned by Anne came immediately to pay homage and to assure her of his loyalty and obedience, so that after scarcely four months Mazarin could note that four provinces, with eighteen strongholds, which had been in the possession of Condé and his adherents, had been brought to loyal allegiance. The only remaining centre of resistance lay far away in the south-west with Bordeaux as the focal point, and the Government was preparing to take the necessary action against it.

On every return to the capital Anne showed her satisfaction by distributing more favours and rewards to her new-found allies, the gentlemen of the Fronde, but the mood in Paris was nevertheless disquieting. Condé's old mother had come to Parlement with a petition in her hands asking for an investigation by the High Court into the alleged misdeeds of the princes, as they had been arbitrarily arrested and imprisoned in violation of the agreement of Rueil. The old Princess was left standing in the lobby with the petition in her hands, since none of the members of Parlement dared to take the document from her, because then the Chamber would have had to deal with the appeal. The princes of royal blood had the hereditary right to take part in the proceedings of Parlement, and if this highest Court Assembly officially confirmed that it had been legal to arrest them and keep them imprisoned without a trial, then all the members of Parlement were exposing themselves to unpredictable hazards. Thus the mood of the House was very apprehensive.

Moreover, the leaders of the Fronde now had definite indications that Mazarin intended to keep his agreements with them only insofar as they suited his own plans. The main test was his promise to obtain the cardinal's hat for Gondi. To all reminders from Mme de Chevreuse his only answer was that the letter with the recommendation to the Pope had to be signed and sent by the Queen herself, and she first wanted to get the consent of her whole Council. In reality, to make this intensely ambitious man Cardinal meant creating a rival to himself, who would spare no effort in trying to take his place in Anne's favour, and he had not the slightest intention of allowing this to happen. He merely instructed his men in Paris to hold out all possible inducements to Mme de Chevreuse, offering her whatever she desired and to try to awaken in her the feeling that Gondi could not be trusted.

Marie was fully aware of the fact that Gondi was dangerous, but because of his influence in Parlement and over the people of Paris he simply had to be kept happy. Besides, his promotion to the rank of cardinal was the basic condition of the agreement with the Fronde and had to be fulfilled. She did not hesitate to warn Mazarin's officials that otherwise Gondi would make common cause with the Minister's enemies whose influence was rising again. As the Court had now moved with the army against Bordeaux, and Paris was again under Gaston's rule, his two chief advisers were Châteauneuf and Gondi, both of whom had managed to win Gaston's confidence. The two distrusted each other, but they were united in their opposition to Mazarin, and Marie, who maintained the best of relations with all three, foresaw that one day Mazarin might be forced to resign. Her candidate to replace him was naturally, as before, Châteauneuf, but when she mentioned this to Gondi he flared up: he would 'not play second fiddle!' Gondi was certainly a dangerous man of unlimited ambition, but he had to be used to contain the despotic trends in the Government, and Marie avoided for the time being any discussion of future plans whilst continuing to urge Mazarin's officials to satisfy Gondi's ambition for a cardinal's hat. That would keep him toeing the line.

One of Mazarin's officials wrote that Mme de Chevreuse had assured him that for some days past she had been suffering the most cruel anxiety, and that her fear of the evils with which the State was threatened prevented her from sleeping; that she had several conversations with the Coadjutor, and had found him very badly disposed towards the Court and full of suspicions of the intentions of the Cardinal; and that, in short, she believed that, to secure his own safety, he would be obliged to make common cause with the enemies of the Cardinal. Mme de Chevreuse had added that she had done everything possible to bring him to a different frame of mind, but without success.

Therefore Mme de Chevreuse continued to insist on the necessity of granting the nomination, pointing out that, by doing so, the Cardinal would assure himself not only of the support of the Coadjutor, but Gaston's as well, over whose mind Gondi was exercising great influence.

In the meantime new events demanded attention: after her rebuff at Le Havre the Duchesse de Longueville continued her journey to Dieppe, was then forced to flee further and had finally reached Flanders, where she managed to make contact with the Archduke Leopold. As at this time the Thirty Years' War in Germany had already come to an end with the Peace of Westphalia, she was able to convince him that with the help of the Condé family a 'just, equitable and reasonable peace' could be achieved between Spain and France as well. Then she recrossed the frontier and won Marshall Turenne to the cause of the arrested princes. They both allied themselves with Spain against Mazarin, and when at the beginning of the summer of 1650 the Spanish offensive from Flanders started, Turenne advanced with a considerable force against Paris. His troops were naturally not strong enough to undertake an attack on the capital, but his intention was immediately apparent: he wanted to take Vincennes and free the princes in order, together with them and all their followers, to continue the fight. It was therefore of the utmost importance that the princes should be taken to a safe place immediately.

Mazarin ordered his officials to transfer them to Le Havre, but that would have meant delivering them entirely into Mazarin's hands, and the Frondeurs opposed this move. They wanted to hold the princes as their hostages against Mazarin in case of need. At the Council meeting under Gaston, Gondi demanded the transfer of the princes to the Bastille, where they would be entirely in the hands of the Fronde. The demand was naturally resisted by all the officials, and finally Mme de Chevreuse, through Châteauneuf and de Laigue, recommended their removal to the castle of Marcoussis, which lay less than twenty miles from Paris and was strong enough to resist an assault. She persuaded Gaston to accept her proposal, and Turenne checked his advance. Instead there now came an envoy from the Archduke Leopold with a letter inviting Gaston to a personal meeting to discuss peace terms. In the streets the envoy's coach was accompanied by crowds cheering the Archduke and Gaston and crying, 'Down with Mazarin!'

Such a meeting would provide evidence that it was Mazarin

alone who was responsible for the continuation of the war, and Gondi, together with Beaufort, urged Gaston to accept the offer. Gaston had already started to prepare for the journey, when his ruling Council, again influenced by Mme de Chevreuse, decided that he and the Archduke alone could not by themselves make any decisions about peace terms as they were 'not sufficiently acquainted with these matters, such being beneath the dignity of their rank'. Instead, Parlement sent a petition to Anne imploring her to bring peace to the realm, menaced by terrible dangers, and to restore the princes to liberty, which Anne recognized as another move against Mazarin.

Marie knew precisely what was going on in Paris behind the scenes: Gondi was pressing Gaston to declare himself regent and to give him Mazarin's position. Marie understood that as long as Mazarin was in power there was no hope of peace, but to have him replaced by Gondi was still more dangerous. Yet Gondi was necessary for dealing with the populace and Parlement, and her efforts to appease him with the appointment to the rank of cardinal brought from Mazarin no more than an assurance that 'he himself desired that Her Majesty might find it possible to accede to the Coadjutor's request'. Thus the attacks against Mazarin continued, and the latest 'Mazarinade' was a picture of him that was hung up in the street on a rope which, passing through two holes, one on either side of the neck, bore the inscription:

'Jules Mazarin – condemned to be hanged for having prevented the accomplishment of peace, for having violated the customs and laws of the country, for having sold all vacant benefices, and for having used sorcery and witchcraft to seduce and dominate the mind of the Queen!'

When soldiers were sent to disperse the laughing and jeering mob, there were riots.

The submission of Bordeaux did not improve the prevailing mood of unrest but only raised the fear of some new deception. In fact, on her return journey, Anne stopped at Fontainebleau, summoned Gaston and forced him to countersign her order for the transfer of the princes from Marcoussis to Le Havre. Only after they had been taken from the vicinity of the capital and were thus out of the reach of the Fronde did she return to Paris, and on the advice of Mazarin she went, not to the Palais Royal, but to the Louvre which had stronger walls and could be better guarded.

As Parlement had now accepted a new petition by Condé's mother and was preparing to discuss the continuing imprisonment of the princes, Anne asked its First President Molé to adjourn the debate until the return of Mazarin, who had gone with the troops to supervise the siege of Rethel in the Ardennes, recently taken by Turenne with Spanish help. Although the official debate was for the time being postponed, Mazarin's rule, with its continuation of Richelieu's policy, evoked increasing hatred, and Gondi's inflammatory speeches in Parlement gained wider and wider approval. Feelings were running so high that Marie foresaw the possibility of decisive action against Mazarin, which would lead to his downfall, and she determined to sound out the Queen as to what her reactions would be in the event of his enforced retirement. On one of her visits to the Louvre she remarked that the Cardinal was a singularly unfortunate man as he incurred blame,

> 'equally for what he did as for the things which he omitted to do, and she herself was astonished to see how much he was hated by the people, so that nothing he did could please or was appreciated. Therefore so long as the Queen retained him in her service, she would continue to be unhappy and there would be difficulties'.

Anne flew into a rage, but as usual Marie had her advice ready at once. The Cardinal should go away for a while until 'the storm had quietened down', then, after some time, agreement for his return could certainly be reached. In reality, Marie believed, as she indicated to her friends, that once Mazarin was away Anne would soon forget him.

The result was that Anne wrote to Mazarin at once, describing this discussion; fearful of approaching danger, she asked him to return to Paris immediately. As Rethel had just been retaken, Mazarin came back and found himself faced with a declaration by Parlement concerning the continuation of the imprisonment of the princes without trial, intimating that this was a violation of the Queen's own decree, which had become law. Anne replied that if the Duchesse de Longueville and Turenne submitted and surrendered the stronghold of Stenay which they held, and when all other rebels had laid down their arms and reaffirmed their loyalty, she would grant a general amnesty – a reply which did not satisfy anybody.

In fact the friends and closest associates of the princes had conceived a plan to bring about their liberation. They contacted Mme de Longueville at Stenay; she, too, was convinced that Mazarin would never resign himself to a reconciliation with the party of the princes, so the only alternative was to open negotiations with the nobles of the Fronde. First of all, Gaston's jealousy of Mazarin had to be aroused. It was also necessary to win over Mme de Chevreuse by offering her terms which could not fail to be attractive to her. What was proposed was no less than the marriage of her daughter Charlotte to Condé's brother Conti. Mme de Longueville agreed to this suggestion. As she wrote in her reply: 'It is therefore to this that we must adhere, if that is possible. . . . In short, I counsel this marriage, and if it is desired, I will even subscribe to it. Her future husband will place her in a position where she need not fear slander.'

Negotiations began and soon an agreement was reached that Mazarin should be deposed and replaced by Châteauneuf as First Minister. Gaston, whom Marie undertook to win to the cause, would remain at the head of the State Council with greater powers and the right to dismiss or appoint its members. Gaston's young daughter by his second marriage, still a child, should be betrothed to Condé's son of the same age, while Condé's brother Conti should marry Charlotte and become Governor of Provence. Condé himself would regain Guyenne, and Gondi would be made a cardinal.

This agreement was finally drawn up and solemnly signed on January 30, 1651. It was in complete accord with Marie's aims. She did not want lawlessness or even rule by Parlement. From the beginning her desire had been to re-establish the old traditional order, namely a community of great nobles who had ruled over the different provinces of the realm with which they had intimate connections. Each of them of course had owed allegiance to the King as the leader of the nobility but not as their absolute master. Richelieu, who had done so much to destroy this old order, had himself waged a long war in the neighbouring German lands to reduce the power of the Emperor and to secure the position of the smaller princes in their own lands. If it was just and right to preserve the peculiarities and traditional customs of the various German principalities, why destroy the customary order in France to make some incidental favourite the omnipotent master over the whole kingdom? Thus the first necessity for the nobility was to combine in a union strong enough to compel the King, or for the time being the Regent, to listen to and to comply with their legitimate wishes.

The present understanding and the agreement recently concluded was proof that the consortium of princes agreed with her ideas; the combination of the houses of Orléans, Condé and Guise would mean the formation of a front of nobles able to resist any kind of pressure; and as Beaufort, the son of the Duc de Vendôme, also stood at the head of the Fronde, the enmity between the Condés and the Vendômes could certainly be overcome at last, which would still further increase the power of the nobles' front.

The conspirators did not waste time. On the very next day Parlement asked for the release of the princes, and two days later Gaston approached Anne demanding the dismissal of Mazarin. A wild and furious scene followed. Anne immediately called Mazarin, and he declared that if King Charles of England had not sacrificed his Minister, Strafford, to the demands of the earl's enemies he, the King, would still be alive and sitting on his throne. Conditions in France could very easily come to resemble those in England: 'Our Kingdom already has its Cromwell in Gondi and its Fairfax in Beaufort!' Anne confirmed everything Mazarin said and ended with the threat that she would let all enemies of the Cardinal 'taste the might of the crown'. Gaston rushed away, declared to his secretary that he would never again 'place himself in the power of this raging harpy' and sent Anne a message through Châteauneuf that he 'would never set foot in the palace again so long as the Cardinal remained there, because he perceived that Mazarin would ruin the realm'.

Next day, Gondi reported Gaston's experiences to Parlement, which decided to summon Mazarin and instruct him to render an explanation for his 'maladministration, arbitrariness and malversations' with the intention afterwards of passing a decree ordering his perpetual exile from the realm. Gaston, as the Lieutenant-General of France, issued a formal interdiction to all military commanders to obey any other orders than those coming from him and the same decree was sent to the Provost of Paris, whereupon barricades were set up in the streets again at once.

The situation became so tense that Anne and Mazarin recalled Marie's advice that the Cardinal should go away for a while. Mazarin declared at the meeting of the Royal Council that, as so many people were demanding that he should be exiled, he could no longer serve the King, and he asked for permission to leave France. Anne gave him the required permission, and on the night of February 6, 1651, he left the palace by a side door and, dressed as a horseman, rode away.

Mazarin's nocturnal flight from Paris was hailed by the Fronde as a complete victory. When Châteauneuf reported the result of the meeting to Gondi, the Coadjutor called out enthusiastically: 'A magnificent political achievement on the part of Mme de Chevreuse to cause the Cardinal to ruin himself!'

But that had certainly not been the intention of Anne and Mazarin. Though Parlement banished him next day from France, he had actually ridden with an escort of 400 riders to St Germain. According to their plan, Anne was to use his absence to make peace with Gaston and then escape with Louis to St Germain where Mazarin would be waiting for them. From there all three would join forces with the army and then deal with the rebels. In any case, as a precautionary measure, Anne had provided him with a document ordering the commander of Le Havre to open the gates of the fortress to him and his escort, which would place the princes in his power.

Next morning, Anne sent a courier to Gaston, asking him to come to the palace, as Mazarin was no longer there. He answered that he was just about to go to Parlement and would come after the session. But Parlement distrusted the Cardinal's sudden flight and Gaston confirmed the edict ordaining Mazarin's banishment from France. Then he sent a declaration to Anne that he would not come to see her until the princes were released.

In the evening of the next day Anne ordered that her coach should be kept ready and issued some personal instructions to her guardsmen. These unusual moves were immediately reported to Châteauneuf, who rushed to Mme de Chevreuse. Marie drove straightaway to Gondi who was asleep, whereupon she ordered his servants to wake him and to ask him to hurry to Gaston, while she herself drove on to the Palais du Luxembourg.

As usual Gaston hesitated about taking any steps, and so the two decided to act on their own. Gondi directed his followers to run through the streets with the cry: 'They are stealing our King! Long live the King! Help!' At two o'clock in the morning, whilst Anne's coach was waiting at the garden entrance, the palace was surrounded and at the gates of the Louvre an armed crowd under the leadership of Beaufort and other commanders demanded entry. Anne realized that her plan to flee had become impracticable and, pretending to have been asleep and only awakened by the tumultuous noise, had the commanders brought to her bedroom. She feigned complete innocence of any secret intentions and at their request let them see the little Louis, also in bed and pretending to be asleep.

In the morning Gaston finally decided to take responsibility for the events in the capital; he ordered all the gates of Paris to be seized by the militia and had the Louvre guarded by armed men. To prevent Anne's escape by river, he moored barges with armed crews at intervals on the Seine. Anne was now a prisoner in the Louvre, not able even to send information to Mazarin, so she signed the order for the release of the princes without further resistance.

After two days of vain waiting at St Germain, Mazarin left and sped to Le Havre. But in spite of the order signed by the Queen, the commander of the fortress refused to let him and his soldiers in. Then an express courier arrived with the information that an authorized delegation was on its way to Le Havre to give the princes their freedom, and he brought a note from Anne to Mazarin, too, saying that he should undertake nothing rash nor resist the princes' liberation as her own safety was at stake. She feared she might be incarcerated in a convent.

Thus Mazarin's plan to get the princes into his power was also frustrated. He therefore asked the commander for permission to see the princes alone, without any escort. This was granted and he hastened to inform them that the Queen had awarded them their freedom and that she had dismissed him because it was believed that their imprisonment had been due to him. He assured them that in reality he had every sympathy with them and that he wished to be the first to bring them the welcome news of their release. But all his protestations of goodwill, all his assertions that their imprisonment had been engineered by the Fronde whilst he had nothing to do with it, all the advice he lavished on them as to whom they must handle with caution, were met by the princes with contempt and disdain. So he made off and left Le Havre, this time in unmistakable flight.

Nor did the princes, who, after more than a year of imprisonment, were so unexpectedly informed of their freedom, waste any time. They rode in all haste in the direction of Paris. On the way they met the delegation sent to Le Havre and were given the details of all that had happened. In St Denis they were welcomed by Gaston, Beaufort and Gondi with an appropriate retinue. Condé displayed the greatest amiability, even embraced Gondi and assured him of his friendship. When three days after their departure from Le Havre they arrived in Paris, they paid a visit to Anne in the Louvre, where, feigning an indisposition, she received them lying in bed, while Louis and his small brother stood by her bedside.

Next came a great reception in Gaston's Palais du Luxembourg, at which, naturally, Mme de Chevreuse and her daughter Charlotte were present. Condé thanked her for all her efforts to obtain his freedom, which he would not have secured without her help. When he mentioned that they were about to be related through the marriage of his brother Conti to her daughter, she replied that promises given in prison did not need to be kept, as they were entered into under duress. He was free to take back his word and act entirely as he pleased. But Conti was immediately captivated by Charlotte's beauty and fell in love with her, and, on his next visit to the Hôtel de Chevreuse, Condé as a free man asked for Charlotte's hand in marriage for his brother, and Marie replied that 'this proposal was a great honour for her family'.

She immediately began to prepare her palace for the wedding festivities, and as Mazarin's possessions had been confiscated after his flight and were being sold as ill-gotten gains, she bought three of his magnificent Italian Gobelins to adorn her house. However, at the drafting of the marriage contract a certain degree of blood relationship between Conti and Charlotte was discovered which necessitated a Papal dispensation, and the marriage had to be postponed until this could arrive from Rome.

Meanwhile a new Government was formed. The Parlement gave Condé a festive reception when he attended, and thus a new Fronde emerged with the inclusion of the princes and their supporters. The vision of Mme de Chevreuse, namely the creation of a united front of the nobility, albeit with the addition of the upper strata of the bourgeoisie in Parlement, seemed to have come about. Gondi proposed that Condé and Gaston should declare themselves joint regents, but as seven months later Louis, on reaching the age of thirteen, was according to tradition due to be declared of age, Gaston refused to proclaim a new regency, so as not to intensify Anne's hatred or, under her influence, that of Louis as well. Thus a new Government Council alone was formed, under the leadership of Gaston and Condé, with Beaufort and Gondi as members, while Châteauneuf was confirmed as Keeper of the Great Seal. Otherwise the positions remained in the hands of Mazarin's old officials and Anne retained the title of Queen-Regent. Now the Civil Guard could be dissolved and the watch on the palace suspended. And the first thing that the Queen did was to restore contact with Mazarin.

Chapter XI

Mazarin's flight from Le Havre had led him through Dieppe and northern France to Bar-le-Duc and then over the frontier into the bishopric of Liège, where he remained for nearly a month until he finally found refuge in the Bishop's Palace at Brühl. But during his journey he had received from Anne a full account of events in Paris and the promise, in the name of Louis, of his recall whenever the authority of the crown was re-established. In addition she assured him that she would not bestow any grace or benefit without his approval and that she would continue to consult him about everything. Thus Marie's belief that Anne would soon forget Mazarin once he was out of the country, proved to have been mistaken.

Besides practical advice, their correspondence revealed the strength of their feelings for each other. Mazarin wrote from Brühl:

'Mon Dieu! How happy I should be, and how satisfied you would feel, if you could see my heart, or if I could describe what is in it! You would not find it difficult, in that case, to agree that never was there a friendship approaching that which I entertain for you. I confess to you that I little imagined that it would go so far as to deprive me of all contentment when my time is employed in anything other than thinking of you. I also wish that I had the power to express my hatred of those indiscreet persons who unceasingly strive to make you forget me and to hinder us from meeting again. . . . They are mistaken if they hope to see in us the effects of absence. . . . Write to me, I entreat you, and say if I shall see you, and when: for this state of things cannot last, even if I should perish. . . .

Anne's letters are just as revealing when she concludes one with the passionate cry, 'I am thousand times yours until the last sigh. Adieu, I can wait no more, and you know why.' Or another: 'I pray you to believe that I shall be always what I should be, come what may.'

So from Liège and afterwards from Brühl there began a constant service of express messengers to and from Anne. To keep himself informed on all political currents and cross-currents, Mazarin by no means forgot his trusted adherents who had remained in the government posts which they had held hitherto. In this way he received exact information about everything that happened at Court and used this to give the Queen precise instructions on how to act in every situation.

One of his first recommendations to Anne was to get on the best possible terms with Condé. In the beginning, Condé played only a minor role, as the Government was in the hands of Gaston and his advisers; but knowing Condé's character, Mazarin had no doubt that a split between them would come soon. One had only to play on the pride of the Prince.

This sudden harmony between the highest nobility was not natural. Mazarin regarded it as one of Mme de Chevreuse's ideas and he raved against her, making the wildest accusations which he knew could not be true and describing her as guilty of actions which she could never have committed:

'She has broken everything to pieces and set everything in motion to entice men from the King's service, to take fortresses by surprise, to raise the Huguenots in revolt and establish them at La Rochelle with the help of Spain; she has always been in the pay of the Spaniards, who gave her money for services she rendered to them! She has done all she could in the interests of Spain and of the Duke of Lorraine at France's expense in order to ruin the Queen and overthrow the State!'

The prospect of a union of the houses of Condé, Orléans, Guise-Lorraine and possibly also Vendôme terrified him. He wrote to Anne:

'The safety of the State and of Your Majesties depends upon the disunion of these princes, since then Your Majesty, by choosing the one whom You judge the most suitable, could lay down the law to the others and work with success for the re-establishment of the royal authority!'

This solidarity of the highest families in the land had to be prevented at any cost and since Mazarin could not find any other grounds, he brought forward arguments of moral conduct:

'I cannot understand how Mme de Longueville, who has such influence on her brother, the Prince de Condé, could give her consent to this marriage. As the affair is well known in all Paris, it seems to me impossible that the very people who should have such a great interest in making the whole thing intolerable to the Prince, should be ignorant of the fact that Gondi visits Mlle de Chevreuse alone every night and has a much more intimate association with her than a man betrothed to her might find desirable.'

The reference that involved Mme de Longueville was well calculated. Her own behaviour was by no means irreproachable: it was rumoured that, before Gondi had been captivated by Charlotte's charms she herself had had a love affair with him. Her husband no longer lived with her. Although she had given her approval to the agreement in order to get the princes free, after her return from Stenay, where she had fought against the Government with Spanish help, she was of the opinion that promises given under the pressure of circumstances need not be kept. Moreover, the proposed marriage of her younger brother Conti, who was completely under her influence, would affect her own position: as Princesse de Condé, Charlotte would have precedence everywhere, at Court and before the Queen, over Mme de Longueville herself, a mere duchess. Under the influence of her mother, Mme de Chevreuse, Charlotte could even become a rival to her in her own family.

This marriage had therefore to be prevented, and as her taunts about Charlotte's association with Gondi failed to make the necessary impression on Conti, who was in love, she began to work on her other brother, Condé himself. The connection with the house of Chevreuse would bring nothing but difficulties and complications, she said. Conti would immediately be drawn into the Orléans circle, which would weaken the interest of the Condés. It was Mme de Chevreuse who was the dominant personality in that circle; she influenced Gaston not only personally but also through Gondi, Beaufort and Châteauneuf, and her actions were incalculable. Yes, it was she who had achieved the release of the princes, but the original idea of arresting them and of Mazarin's collaboration with the Fronde had likewise been hers. Châteauneuf, the man who had obtained the death sentence upon the Duc de Montmorency continued to be her friend, and she had managed to make him Keeper of the Great Seal again. She had always been a partisan of the house of Vendôme, the rivals of the Condés.

It was not long before Condé began to share his sister's apprehensions and to curtail his visits to the Hôtel de Chevreuse. Moreover, as Anne, on Mazarin's instructions to do everything possible to win over Condé, had promised to return to him the governorship of Guyenne, which she had just retaken from his adherents with utmost difficulty, and in addition offered the governorship of the Provence to Conti, the Prince soon began to imagine himself the most important person in the kingdom, and he did not like the attitude of the Fronde. Anne decided to find out whether a break between them could be brought about. On April 3rd, scarcely six weeks after Condé's release, and after consultation with him alone, she instructed one of Mazarin's men in the Council to demand the return of the Great Seal from Châteauneuf: that meant removing him from the Government.

Châteauneuf's sudden dismissal without prior information to Gaston, who presided over her Council, was a carefully considered move to test the strength and cohesion of the different groups in the Fronde. As Châteauneuf was the only man of the Fronde actively serving in the Government, an excited meeting took place next day at the Palais du Luxembourg, at which wild suggestions followed one upon the other: the populace should be called upon to rise and march against the royal palace; Anne should be deposed, the ministers thrown out of the windows, and the King taken away. But all these proposals were empty talk, revealing the prevailing confusion, and Condé, who of course was present, declared contemptuously he would not make 'war with chamber-pots and cobble-stones'. If Gaston decided to resort to arms he himself would retire to Burgundy and raise an army there while Monsieur (as the King's brother was usually styled) could have the honour of leading the populace of Paris. In his arrogance he let the leaders of the Fronde know that he did not disapprove of Châteauneuf's dismissal, and so the split between him and the other groups of the

169

Fronde, which Mazarin had hoped for from the beginning, became evident.

That was the opportunity for the next step, the prevention of that dreaded union of the greatest of the noble families. Regarding himself as Anne's first adviser, and having regained his vast possessions, Condé now inclined more and more to his sister's opinion that the connection with the house of Chevreuse meant a lowering of his own status: but as he had been a free man when he had mistakenly asked for Charlotte's hand for his brother, his problem was to find a way out which would not reflect upon his honour and brand him as a man who breaks his word. He greatly welcomed it, therefore, when Anne told him of her doubts about this marriage, naturally without mentioning that her reason was her fear of increasing the power of the feudal nobility. It was sufficient for him that she said, 'This marriage is not opportune,' and, in the name of the twelve-year-old Louis, as the head of the Bourbons, she refused to permit it.

Now the only question was how to convey this breach of promise to Mme de Chevreuse. Condé charged one of the presidents of Parlement with this task. When this representative of the highest court went to the Hôtel de Chevreuse on April 15th, two weeks after Châteauneuf's dismissal, he found Mme de Chevreuse in the salon with Charlotte, who was finishing her toilet in front of the fire, and Gondi. He evidently felt extremely embarrassed and found it very difficult to produce the right explanation. He conveyed kindest regards from the princes and the assurance that they were inconsolable at this setback, but hoped that, given time, they would get the Queen's agreement to the marriage; thus 'the matter should be regarded only as temporarily postponed and not broken off.'

Charlotte burst into disdainful laughter, and although Marie remained outwardly quiet and polite, inside she was seething. What did these people think? Did they think she would believe that Condé could be influenced in his actions in the least by any objection or opposition from Anne? Condé's repudiation of the proposed marriage meant nothing less than that he rejected the establishment of a united front of the nobility, which was her main aim. The man whom she had helped out of prison for this purpose now saw the way open for his own elevation and wanted to keep his future power for himself, without being involved in any agreements which could bind him. The united front of the nobles would restrict his freedom of action as he would have to consider the interests and aspirations of the others, while if he got to the top alone he could do absolutely as he wished. He would establish a new despotic rule, perhaps still stronger and more severe than Mazarin's or even Richelieu's had been. They knew that they depended completely on the will of the monarch and that if they lost the King's favour they would sink without trace, while Condé would remain a Bourbon prince who did not mind insulting other great families, as he was now doing to hers.

That was not the purpose for which she had fought Mazarin and forced him to flee. This personal insult cried out for revenge. Five days after the breaking off of the engagement she instructed one of Mazarin's officials in the Government to write to the Cardinal that he should direct the Queen to place complete confidence in her and to follow her advice; this would be of great advantage to him.

Mazarin received this message with extraordinary pleasure. He had already been feeling very anxious about his own future. The split in the Fronde had not brought the results which he had expected. The party of the Prince alone was now stronger then the whole Fronde had ever been, and Condé continued his campaign against Mazarin with undiminished zeal. He declared in Parlement that the Cardinal was maintaining his influence in the Government through the continual use of couriers. Mazarin had complained to Anne that he was without money, and Condé demanded an investigation into the activity of a Roman banker who had just left France with an enormous sum. Thus, of late, Mazarin had already started to modify his recommendations to Anne. Contrary to his previous advice to make common cause with Condé, he was now warning her not to trust the Prince and not to satisfy his ever-increasing demands for further positions of power for his relatives and adherents, but nevertheless to take care not to offend him, as he was now beginning to fear what the Prince might do.

Under these circumstances Mme de Chevreuse's offer to work in his interest seemed like a blessing. After the receipt of this news he immediately wrote to one of his trusted men in the Government: 'I am convinced that Mme de Chevreuse and her adherents will do everything in their power to take revenge on the princes.' A corresponding instruction went out to Anne too and very soon Marie was called by the Queen to a confidential meeting.

Anne asked her openly whether she was prepared to help her to take revenge on their common enemy, and Marie replied, 'The blood of the Bourbons shall wipe off the stain which it has inflicted on the honour of Lorraine.' They came to a complete agreement about the action to be undertaken and a few days later Gondi was sent for and received by the Queen. He swore solemnly to be loyal to her and to act in her service, and then started a campaign against Condé in Parlement. But as he also continued to speak against Mazarin, Anne reproached him and received the reply that, as Mazarin was so strongly hated by everybody, he himself, if he showed publicly that he was not against the Cardinal, would become suspect in the eyes of other Frondeurs and lose his influence in Parlement and with the people and so be unable to help her. In public he must therefore maintain his opposition to Mazarin and be considered his enemy. But what he could do in her service would be to compel Condé to leave Paris and also to bring Gaston back to her.

Anne still had her doubts about making common cause with Gondi and asked Mazarin for advice, but his reply dispersed her apprehensions. He wrote:

'You know that the most bitter enemy I have in the world is the Coadjutor, but it is better to use him than grant Monsieur le Prince what he demands. Give Gondi the cardinalate; if necessary, give him even my apartments in the Palais Royal. He will perhaps be more devoted to Gaston than to Yourself, but Gaston does not aim at ruining the kingdom. If you concede all the Prince's demands, You will have nothing more to do other than to conduct him to Rheims and place the crown on his brow. Madame, I beseech, I implore You, resist such dishonourable, such preposterous demands! . . .'

Nevertheless, he continued to warn her not to alienate the Prince yet by any sudden withdrawal of her favour, but to see that the enmity between Condé and the leaders of the Fronde was maintained. 'For myself, I would rather remain for ever in exile than return to such a precarious situation.'

This letter dispelled Anne's doubts entirely, the more so as

Gondi kept his promise to bring Gaston back to her. He accomplished this by warning Gaston of the danger that would arise if Condé retained any longer his singular influence upon the Queen. Gaston appeared at the palace and a reconciliation took place. Now Anne also fulfilled her promises. The letter to the Pope, recommending Gondi's appointment as Cardinal, was despatched. As Marie and Gondi demanded Châteauneuf's reinstatement in the Government, an even higher position than before was bestowed upon him, by making him Controller of Finances. Lastly, to show her gratitude to Mme de Chevreuse, Anne arranged the betrothal of the now 24-year-old Charlotte to Mancini, Mazarin's seventeen-year-old nephew, promised to appoint him Duc de Rethelois on the marriage, and to provide him with a suitable governorship. As one of the sons of the Duc de Vendôme had just married a niece of Mazarin, and as the other two nieces of the Cardinal were also about to marry into the highest nobility, Marie saw that the creation of a united front of the nobility might still become a reality.

In the meantime the fight between Gondi and Condé in Parlement continued and often led to stormy debates. Derisive pamphlets against Condé started to appear and rumours began to circulate that Mme de Chevreuse was again demanding the arrest of the Prince; if he resisted he might even be killed in the street. Condé himself became anxious when he realized that he was now opposed by Anne, Gaston, the Frondeurs and even by a section of Parlement which took exception to his derogatory remarks. So he fortified his palace, kept an armed retinue there day and night, and travelled through the streets of Paris only with a strong escort of horsemen. Then one night there was an unusual noise and clacking of hooves in the neighbouring streets, as if a regiment of cavalry was approaching the palace, and he became so nervous that he seized a horse and galloped out of Paris to his near-by château of Saint-Maur. From there he wrote a letter to Parlement saying that he had been forced to flee from the capital to avoid unlawful arrest.

When it became established that the clatter of hooves had been caused by a large herd of cattle driven by peasants to the market, there was much derisive laughter in Parlement. Nevertheless the House took action. The moderate majority did not want Gondi playing a dominant role at Court and charged Gaston with the task of travelling to Saint-Maur and bringing Condé back to Paris. When they both returned, Parlement insisted that Condé should visit Anne without delay, at the same time requesting the Queen to dismiss from the Government those of Mazarin's followers who were still in office.

Anne gave Condé a very cool reception and naturally tried to resist Parlement's request: Mazarin was out of the country and these men were experienced officials, the only ones who knew their jobs thoroughly. She complained to Gondi, but received the reply that in spite of her counter-assurances everyone was aware that in fact Mazarin continued to govern as before, and this was the obstacle which ruined all his, Gondi's, efforts. Thus, finally, Anne had to submit to the request, especially as the officials concerned chose to leave Paris rather than await a summons for interrogation.

But in spite of all the problems which beset her, Anne's thoughts were now mainly occupied with the preparation for the most important event of the year, when Louis would, on September 5th, celebrate his thirteenth birthday and be declared of age. Legally, he would then take over the Government, her regency would officially come to an end, and all decrees and orders would be issued in the name of the King direct and carry much more weight. She would no longer have to ask advice from anybody, and the King's advisers would be appointed by himself.

In recognition of the coming official change in the Government, which would label any objection as resistance to the King's orders, Gaston demanded, now in agreement with Condé, and together with the conference of nobles then sitting in Paris, the convocation of the Estates General. He expected to get from this assembly approval to a proposal to delay the declaration of Louis' coming of age until his sixteenth birthday, when he was due to be crowned. It was rumoured that in the event of the continuation of Louis' minority until his coronation he intended to assume the regency himself and to make sure of his influence at Court by appointing Mme de Chevreuse Controller of the Royal Household.

Anne could not refuse the convocation of the Estates General without offending the whole of the nobility and clergy, but she received tacit support from Parlement, which disliked the idea of the convocation, as the majority of its members came from the middle class and belonged to the *noblesse de robe*, and at the Estates General they would, before the whole nation, figure only as representative of the third, the lowest estate. And so, to create more confusion, Anne presented to Parlement a new indictment of Condé, accusing him of attempting to conspire against the crown with the government in Brussels and also of having started to withdraw his military contingents from the royal armies. Condé accused Gondi of being the originator of all these slanders, and as public attention was absorbed by the stormy scenes in Parlement, Anne contrived, without creating a stir, to promise the convocation of the Estates General in September, that is to say not prior to, but after, Louis' birthday. It was a promise that did not bind her, because then the order would have to come from Louis.

Thus, when with magnificent pageantry the proclamation of Louis XIV's majority took place, the whole Condé family was absent. Five days earlier the Prince had left for his provinces in the south-west, ordering Conti and Mme de Longueville to follow him. Although the King, in his first *lit de justice*, acquitted him of all the accusations which had been made against him, proclaiming his innocence, the Prince had no intention of returning to Paris in order to play the part of a courtier, but stayed in his province to continue with his preparations for rebellion. On September 22nd, he made a triumphal entry into Bordeaux, which, in spite of its surrender to Anne and Mazarin the previous year, had remained loyal to him. He assembled his troops there and invaded the neighbouring provinces. The Government found itself forced to leave Paris and to move against him, however unsure it was about the attitude of the Paris population. Molé, now appointed Keeper of the Great Seal, remained in the capital to keep an eye on Gaston and Parlement while the Court, together with the army, made their first move against the territories held by Conti. At the approach of the royal troops Bourges rose against the Prince and was quickly occupied; then the Court moved to Poitiers, which it chose as its residence, and under the command of Turenne, who did not want to participate in a rising against the King, the royal troops invaded the Charente, which Condé had annexed.

The royal army was stronger than Condé's and he was at first defeated; but afterwards a number of encounters took place with varying results, and finally Louis summoned Mazarin back to

France to join him. Immediately after the declaration of his majority, he had written to the Cardinal that he would call him back as soon as circumstances permitted, and Mazarin had instantly left Brühl and begun to recruit mercenaries. In December the call from Poitiers reached him, so he crossed the frontier with 1,000 horsemen and 4,000 infantry, entered Sedan and began a march to Poitiers.

This news rekindled the spirit of the Fronde in Paris. Molé managed to get Parlement to condemn Condé as guilty of high treason, but could not prevent it at the same time declaring Mazarin a 'traitor, a common robber and an enemy of peace in Christendom', setting a price on his head and issuing a circular to all towns and provinces enjoining them to stop his advance and to arrest him. Parlement also wanted to petition the King to forbid the Cardinal's return, but Molé declared that Mazarin was only following the King's orders and that all the previous decrees of Parlement had thus become invalidated. Nevertheless he could not alter the prevailing mood. Gondi now convinced Gaston the time was ripe to form a new government together with Condé, and Gaston began to recruit troops in his part of the country in order to help the Prince in case of need. In the meantime, quite unconcerned, Mazarin marched with his mercenaries through the whole of France to Poitiers, where he arrived at the end of January.

In these circumstances opinion in Paris was completely divided. On the one side a flood of pamphlets appeared, calling all well-meaning Parisians who wanted peace to act against the agitators; on the other hand a wave of furious Mazarinades demanded a rising and a bloodbath. But the great majority of the population, suffering under the pressure of continually rising prices and exhausted by misery and hunger, now wanted nothing but the return of the Court, stating that if the King did not assume full power soon and restore order they would all die of hunger.

In the country the civil war continued. Various encounters took place with no more than limited successes to either side, and Condé decided to take the advice of his adherents in Paris. If he could conquer the capital, his position would be more secure. He managed to by-pass the armies of his opponents and quickly moved to Paris. Once in the city he declared that he had come to protect the capital and Parlement from the Italian usurper who was dominating the King. He won over the populace, formed a government with Gaston at the head, declared himself Supreme Commander and began to organize the defence of the city. Meanwhile, the royal troops under the command of Turenne were approaching and the Court took up residence at St Germain.

Condé's army was numerically weaker than the royal troops and he asked Charles of Lorraine for help, sending him money raised by a special tax in Paris. Charles came with over 6,000 mercenaries and occupied Etampes, which Turenne's troops were besieging. Thereupon Mazarin offered him a still larger sum of money with the promise to raise the siege of Etampes, if he would leave. The Cardinal even gave the undertaking that he would return Lorraine to him, the duchy from which he had been expelled a decade earlier.

Charles took money from both sides and remained in his strategic position, surrounded by fertile country in which his mercenaries could live by plundering and looting. Mazarin urgently appealed to Mme de Chevreuse for help, and Marie was naturally wholeheartedly against Condé's hold on Paris. If Gondi made common cause with him, in spite of the fact that he had recently received the news of his appointment as Cardinal, that would be typical of the man. Gaston was evidently only a puppet in their hands. When Mazarin had marched into France and was on his way to Poitiers, she had written to him saying that she would remain true to their agreement and he could rely on her, and in his answer he had assured her of his friendship. When she now received his appeal for help she did not hesitate. She dressed herself as a peasant woman, drove to Charles' camp at Etampes and managed to reach him. Her sudden appearance and her guarantee that all Mazarin's pledges would be strictly adhered to did not fail to make the necessary impression upon her old friend; Charles signed the agreement to leave France, and four days later, on June 10th, he moved away to Flanders together with his mercenaries and an enormous train of baggage filled with plunder.

The struggle for Paris had now to be fought out between Condé and Turenne. Condé had not enough troops to protect the capital on all sides, while Turenne was in a position to select the point of attack. After some skirmishes, the decisive battle took place three

M

weeks later, on July 2nd, outside the Gate of St Antoine. To distinguish friend from foe, Condé's men displayed a wisp of straw on their hats, while those of Turenne had stuck a piece of paper in theirs. At first Condé proved to be superior, but then Turenne received reinforcements and artillery, and under pressure of his attack Condé, with the remainder of his troops, to whom the Gate of St Antoine was opened, just managed to withdraw into the capital. When the royal cavalry tried to pursue them, the mobilized militia fired a volley of musketry from the city walls, which forced the royalists to retreat. Condé had lost over half of his effective forces, nearly 2,000 men, in the battle; the royal army counted about 4,000 men killed and wounded. Among the latter was Mazarin's nephew Mancini, who was betrothed to Marie's daughter Charlotte. He died two days after the battle.

In spite of his defeat Condé still remained master of Paris. When the civic authorities refused to side with him, the populace stormed the Hôtel de Ville, set fire to the locked doors and burst into the council chambers. Those who did not manage to flee were killed or wounded. The following day Parlement appointed Beaufort as Governor of Paris and declared that Gaston, in spite of the King's majority, should continue as Lieutenant-General of the Realm in order to free Louis from Mazarin's influence. A provisional government was formed, a tax put on all houses, and all gold and silver in the mint was sequestrated. Condé transferred the remainder of his troops to a suburb, where they maintained themselves mainly by plunder.

Assessing the position, Turenne recommended negotiations and withdrew with his army from the suburb of St Denis to Pontoise. The Court followed him and Louis ordered Parlement to attend there for a meeting. But only about two dozen of the members of Parlement answered the call. This meant that, while the Government was unable to subdue the capital, the powers in control of the city refused to obey its orders, although they professed their loyalty to the King himself, and the leaders of the Fronde continued to declare that they were only fighting to break Mazarin's dominance over the boy-king. Thus a compromise had to be reached and the only possible way was to exclude Mazarin from the Government.

Mazarin made Louis issue him with a testimonial which praised his loyalty and devotion and exculpated him from all the accusations made against him, declaring them to be slanderous. Then Mazarin resigned his position and left France for the second time. His 'discharge' removed any pretext for further resistance, and as conditions in the city were by then disastrous the call for the return of the Court became more and more insistent. A pamphlet appeared telling the Parisians:

> 'that the capital had lost one third of its population, most of them having died from hunger and want. The revenues of the Hôtel de Ville remained unpaid, since nearly half of the houses stood empty and the inhabitants of the dwellings still occupied could not pay their rates because trade was at a complete standstill. The merchants could not earn a living; the craftsmen and skilled workers were unemployed and starving; the store-houses for corn, wine, wood and other necessities of life were empty, and the fields around the town remained unploughed and unsown, for the villages were deserted and thus no new crop could be expected.'

The only hope lay therefore in the early return of the Court and the re-establishment of communications with the provinces. Nevertheless, there was still one condition to be fulfilled. Before they would consent to lay down their arms, the nobles demanded that the King should confirm their rights, dignities and previous positions. The Government was prepared to accede to this request and a delegation of the clergy, headed by Gondi, now Cardinal de Retz, came to Compiègne to petition for the return of the King. Although Gondi's speech declaring that the royal house would now be united and rule in peace with Gaston in the Government and Condé as military commander, met with a very cool reception from Anne and her advisers, who had very different intentions, Louis presented him with the cardinal's hat.

As Condé was still in Paris, Louis issued an order to the Parisians to rearm against him, and Condé, who refused to submit, withdrew with his men from the capital. Gaston also left Paris and retired to his residence at Blois; Beaufort, the commander of the militia, fled, and the civic authorities took over the administration. On October 21, 1652, Louis, Anne and the whole Court entered the city in full state and were wildly acclaimed by the populace;

however, the King still thought it prudent to take up residence not in the Palais Royal but in the stronger Louvre. Next day the King summoned Parlement and declared a general amnesty with certain exceptions as in the case of Beaufort and some of the more outspoken Frondeurs, who were banished. Gaston lost his title of Lieutenant-General and was forbidden to leave Blois, and Parlement itself received the order to submit within three days a plea for the King's pardon for its previous behaviour. When it complied with the order and received the royal pardon, it was at the same time instructed that it was no longer to concern itself with political or financial matters.

That was the end of the Fronde, which had first attempted to bring the activities of the royal Government under the control of Parlement in the interest of the nation and then, together with the high nobility, who had been oppressed by Richelieu and Mazarin, started the revolt against the crown. Now there were other men around the King and Anne, such as the Duc de Vendôme, the Duc de Guise, old friends of Mme de Chevreuse but with no pretensions to resist the absolutist tendencies of the monarchy, and apart from them there were only secretaries and officials of Mazarin, mostly upstarts from the third estate. In the name of Louis, the Government declared that the King was prepared to take Condé back into favour if he unreservedly repudiated all his associations with the enemy, but the Prince in his arrogance refused to submit and started new negotiations with Spain. Thereupon an edict was issued, declaring him guilty of high treason and depriving him of all his titles, offices and possessions.

Mme de Chevreuse had had her revenge on Condé, but it was paid for dearly by the death of young Mancini, Mazarin's nephew and Charlotte's fiancé.

Chapter XII

In this changed atmosphere at Court, Mme de Chevreuse was naturally fully accepted. Her daughter Charlotte did not seem to have taken the loss of her betrothed too badly. She had lost nothing of her old gaiety and was as full of spirit as ever, and Marie was certain that she would soon find a new noble suitor for the hand of her daughter among the young courtiers. Then on November 7th, less than three weeks after the return of the Government to Paris, Charlotte suddenly felt ill. Her condition worsened alarmingly. After a few hours she was seized by violent convulsions and died the same day. As one of those present wrote: 'Her death surprised everybody. It was observed how her face and her whole body became completely black in the shortest possible time.'

Had she been poisoned? By whom? Why? This sudden death of the child she had loved best, with whom she had lived inseparably for nearly a decade in Paris, in banishment, in flight and in exile abroad, and for whose future she had cherished such great hopes and made so many plans, hit Marie like a thunderbolt. She did not believe that she could ever recover from the blow which at one stroke had destroyed all her expectations for the future glory of her family. Of her other three daughters, the eldest, by Luynes, had died six years previously from chicken-pox; the other two had been educated in convents during her long periods of absence and had become nuns. One of them had also recently died while the youngest was destined to become Abbess of Jouarre in succession to her aunt, Marie's sister-in-law. Marie's son, the Duc de Luynes, was very pious, 'entirely out of character', as she used to say, and lived with his wife and four children in complete retirement in a small mansion he had built for himself near a Jansenist monastery.

In addition to the surrender of all her hopes for her family, Marie had by now recognized that her cherished design of creating a united front of the nobility was nothing but an empty dream. The old nobility, which had been prepared to risk possessions and life for the traditional freedoms and customs of their feudal lands, no longer existed. The Fronde had not developed into the kind of movement that it promised when Mme de Chevreuse plunged into it with all her energy and became its heart and soul. Every noble-man who joined it had thought of nothing but his own advantage, hoping either to obtain a bigger income, or a higher status for himself at Court or, as Condé, to establish a dictatorial rule of his own.

The monarchy was victorious in every direction. The whole nobility pledged obedient service to the Crown. The continuously falling value of the money which they received as feudal dues in amounts fixed long before had made them increasingly dependent upon royal favour, which alone could dispense honours, pensions and sinecures. The people, too, after the misery which the civil war had brought not only to Paris but also to large parts of the country, longed above all for stability and order. When new financial demands were put before Parlement and Gondi, now Cardinal de Retz, made a speech in his customary provocative manner, he received the usual, very gracious welcome on his next visit to Court, and was then immediately arrested and taken to Vincennes; but neither the populace nor any group of nobles or faction of Parlement made the slightest move on his behalf.

Mazarin wrote to the fifteen-year-old Louis XIV, 'You have it in you to become the most glorious King that France has ever had,' and shortly afterwards Louis recalled Mazarin to Paris. As a contemporary writer noted: 'This banished man, this disturber of public tranquillity, this obstruction to world peace on whose head a premium had been put, returned to the capital and his reappear-ance not only failed to cause a rising, but he was greeted as a victorious hero, covered with glory.'

Everybody at Court rushed to visit him and the nobles told Anne that the whole of France was on his side. They had good reason for this: Mazarin had found in Fouquet a man to whom the rich bourgeoisie were prepared to lend money which, after ample deductions for himself, he passed on to the Government as a loan. The Court now had money, and a royal edict ordered the re-opening of the Chamber of Finance, which meant the beginning of the payment of long-delayed arrears and interest on loans.

When, two years later, Fouquet imposed still heavier taxes on the country and Parlement demanded an investigation of the decree, Louis XIV, now seventeen, gave a first indication of his character. He was out hunting when he received the message from Mazarin, and so he rode in all haste to Paris, entered the Chamber in his hunting clothes and declared: 'I have specially come here to forbid you to discuss the decree, and to prohibit you, Mister President, to allow this, however much the gentlemen may press you.' Otherwise he left the government of the country completely to Mazarin, and Mazarin's only concession to Parlement was to inform them that the war was the cause of the new tax burdens, since the fight against Spain and Condé, now in open alliance with them, continued with both failures and successes, and Mazarin even concluded an agreement with Cromwell specifying that the English were to send a fleet and 6,000 soldiers for the siege of Dunkirk and Gravelines, in return for which England was promised Dunkirk after its fall.

Immediately on his return Mazarin wrote a letter full of praise to Mme de Chevreuse, expressing his hope that she would keep him in kind remembrance. He also sent Colbert to her, his trusted friend and a high official usually chosen for delicate tasks, and Colbert reported to him: 'I have visited all the persons Your Eminence commended to me; Mme de Chevreuse told me of the great pleasure which Your Eminence had given her with the honour of your affectionate remembrance.' Marie herself wrote to him assuring him that she would use every opportunity to prove how near to her heart his interests were, and that he could always call on her whenever he needed.

That was an easy promise, as at the peak of his power, without a rival, in the favour of both Louis and Anne, and with all his enemies removed, what possible need could he have of her? Now she had lost all interest in events at Court and in the Government. Naturally she had free access to Anne at any time, but she only went when it was necessary for reasons of courtesy or if she wanted to put in a good word for a friend. She was now fifty-three years old, had become very corpulent and often felt tired. Nevertheless, she had not lost her innate ability nor her old power of persuasion, and she proved it when suddenly a call came from Mazarin. Condé was now with his troops in the south near Provence, where the young Duc de Noirmoutier was Governor; Mazarin feared they might join forces, so he asked for Marie's help to prevent this. The Duc de Noirmoutier had been a fervent admirer of Charlotte's charms and a frequent visitor at the Hôtel de Chevreuse; Marie went to see him, and a few talks and meetings between them were sufficient to persuade him to enter the royal service instead of joining up with Condé.

Having proved to Mazarin that he could rely on her word, she retired with her devoted lover de Laigue to Dampierre, largely occupied with her own complicated financial affairs, and came to Paris mainly when her numerous lawsuits demanded it. She had to start proceedings against her father, the aged Duc de Montbazon, not only for her share in her mother's inheritance but also for the dowry and the annuity which he had promised her on her marriage and which she had never received. When the courts pronounced in her favour he transferred various possessions to her; however, when she wanted to take them over, they proved to be already mortgaged to various of his creditors. When he died the next year, 1654, at the age of eighty-six, it became evident that everything he possessed was in some way pledged, and to cover the funeral costs even the furniture had to be sold. The Duc de Montbazon had assigned some of his official honours and offices to his son, but when Marie asked for part of the income from these sources her brother claimed the rights of priority, which led her into protracted and unsuccessful litigation.

Her financial wrangles with her husband were still more intricate. He paid not the slightest attention to the judgement of Parlement, given sixteen years earlier, granting her the separation of property, an annuity and the Hôtel de Chevreuse. He gave her no money, continued to live in the Hôtel de Chevreuse and took advantage of the separation of property by directing his creditors to her, although she could only pay them with letters of credit, thus mortgaging the future payments which she expected from him. In the end she wrote to the Chancellor Séguier, telling him that all her possessions were the 400,000 francs which her husband owed her, of which he had given her nothing but a letter of credit.

Finally, their lawyers came to an agreement whereby her husband sold her the Duchy of Chevreuse, including the château at Dampierre and the estate attaching to it, but he retained for himself the title of Duke and the right to live at Dampierre. Marie's son, the Duc de Luynes, managed to arrange the necessary mortgages and the price to be paid to her husband was immediately used for the payment of his debts. Then Marie had to take the oath of service before the Chancellor Séguier for 'the Duchy with all its belongings and dependencies'.

Early in the next year, 1657, her husband succumbed to a stroke. Despite the financial wrangles, despite his numerous love affairs as well as her own, despite the long years of separation and her deep political involvement, in which he took no share, their relationship had on the whole remained one of toleration, acceptance and friendship. After his death, which occurred at Dampierre, it became evident that all the income, the rents and various dues from the Duchy were insufficient to maintain the Hôtel de Chevreuse in Paris as well as Dampierre, and Marie decided to sell her residence in the capital, which not so long ago had been a brilliant centre of political activity and the scene of many of her triumphs. Now, when she had to go to Paris, she had to find lodgings, or a house to rent, and therefore, to enable her to live in a style befitting her status, the King granted her the revenues of the County of Charolais and another barony.

At this time peace negotiations were proceeding between France and Spain, in the course of which Spain, now completely exhausted, had to accept one by one the conditions dictated by Mazarin. He was the victor, and this victory led to the hegemony of France in Europe. For the last five years he had been the undisputed ruler of the country, yet it is remarkable that, in spite of all these achievements, he could not forget for a moment the conspiracies and tribulations of the past. During the peace negotiations he said to the Spanish Minister:

'You are most fortunate! In your country, as in all others, you have two types of women: an abundance of coquettes and a few decent women. The first type think of nothing but how to satisfy their lovers, and the second of nothing but how to please their husbands. In both cases their only aspiration is the gratification of their vanity and their desire for luxury. But our ladies, on the contrary, whether they are virtuous or loose, old or young, clever or foolish, all want to interfere in everything! An honest woman will not go to sleep with her husband, nor will a loose one with her lover, unless he has first told her something about the affairs of the day. They must know everything, see everything, be informed about everything and, what is even worse, they must meddle in everything and mix everything up. We have some of them here who daily throw us into a worse mess than there ever was in Babylon. We have here some who are capable of governing three great kingdoms or of overturning them, like the Duchesse de Longueville or the Duchesse de Chevreuse.'

It was not long after the conclusion of the Treaty of the Pyrénées and Louis' subsequent marriage to his cousin, the Infanta Maria Theresa, a daughter of Philip IV of Spain, that Mme de Chevreuse was provoked once more to take action. When peace was concluded, Charles of Lorraine came to Paris demanding the fulfilment of the promise made to him of the return of Lorraine, but he met with deaf ears everywhere, and so Marie went to his aid with all her old drive and tenacity. She did not cease to remind Mazarin that it was on his word that she had guaranteed Charles the return of his country and it was because of her pledge that he left France. She did not relax until Mazarin finally fulfilled his promise to return Lorraine to Charles, although on condition that the fortresses should be razed and that French troops should have the right of passage.

Mme de Longueville, on her part, had long since abandoned all resistance and had again become one of Anne's ladies-in-waiting, while her brother Conti married one of Mazarin's nieces. As the Spaniards, in spite of having to accept many humiliating conditions, had remained unshakable on one point, the reinstatement of Condé in all his former titles and possessions, the Prince had now returned to France and had become an obedient courtier.

The whole atmosphere at Court had changed considerably. There were no more political problems to discuss, no centres of resistance to overcome, nor new ones to be formed. When Mazarin, who had been very ill for a long time, died in March 1661 at the age of fifty-nine, there was not even any question of competing for his post, for the 22-year-old Louis XIV at once declared that there would be no new appointment and that he himself was taking over the Government. Thus all the gossip at Court centred around existing or prospective love affairs, particularly those of the King.

Mme de Chevreuse, again unintentionally, provided new material for this kind of scandal-mongering. Four years earlier, shortly after the death of the Duc de Chevreuse, the Duchesse de Montbazon, second wife of Marie's father, had died suddenly from a relapse after an attack of measles and Marie took the youngest of the Duchess's daughters, seventeen-year-old Anne de Rohan, whom she had always much liked, into her care. But Marie's son, the Duc de Luynes, who for a few years had been a widower, became fascinated by the great beauty of his step-aunt, eighteen years younger than himself, and wanted to marry her. Marie was profoundly shocked by the idea of such a marriage, but he persisted in his demand and finally after years of refusal, Marie had to relent in order to prevent him from retiring into religious solitude. Anne, who in the meantime had entered a convent as a novice, was persuaded to abandon her idea of becoming a nun; a papal dispensation for the marriage was obtained, and when Marie then duly introduced her step-sister, who had now become her daughter-in-law, at Court there was an immediate reaction. The Court Jester, Bussy-Rabutin, declared that:

'Mme de Chevreuse, now only the monument of all the pleasures for which her body had once been the temple, had, as she could no longer get anything for herself, introduced the Duchesse de Luynes, the most beautiful woman of France, into our world in order to replace Mlle de la Vallière in the heart of Louis XIV.'

This jest could not fail to delight the Court, as the liaison between the King and Mlle de la Vallière was supposed to be a strictly guarded secret. The courtiers were watching and guessing who next might gain his favour. However, the new Duchesse de Luynes took no part in the life of the Court but lived quietly and very happily with her husband.

Marie used the occasion of her appearance at Court to remind Queen Anne of a long-standing promise to visit her in Dampierre. Mazarin had recently died, which meant that Anne had time to spare, and when the summer came she went with Henriette-Marie, the fugitive Queen of England, and other ladies for a stay of several days. It was said afterwards that during this visit long and serious conferences took place. If the ladies discussed their experiences and the changes since Anne, as a fourteen-year-old princess had arrived in France to be married to Louis XIII and Marie became her lady-in-waiting, they could not have lacked topics for conversation, but it seems that the prevailing situation and decisions about the future occupied their thoughts still more. Since the death of Mazarin Anne had become very lonely; she was no longer needed even for ceremonial occasions, and Louis, as the absolute ruler, disliked any interference in State affairs. Thus she had nothing to do and her days were empty. Overcome by her feeling of uselessness, she decided to retire from the world into the convent of Val-de-Grâce.

Marie, on the contrary, was still very much concerned with the events of the day. The mood in the country was not at all happy because of the manoeuvres of Fouquet, the Minister of Finance. Anne favoured Fouquet very much, because under his administration there was always enough cash available for all the needs of the Court, and so Marie could not resist the temptation of describing to the Queen the sharp practices by which he allowed the treasury only a fraction of the money which he borrowed or extorted, keeping an inordinate share for himself and mortgaging the country's future income. When, two months later, just after the sumptuous inauguration of his newly built palace, Fouquet was dismissed and arrested, the gossip at Court did not fail to ascribe his downfall to Marie's intervention, particularly as his office was given to Colbert, who for over a decade and a half had been the contact between Mme de Chevreuse and Mazarin and who was *au fait* with all her interests and difficulties.

In spite of the sale of the Hôtel de Chevreuse in Paris and the additional income granted her by the King, Marie found that as the result of the continuous devaluation of money and ever-rising prices the maintenance of Dampierre, with all the necessary staff, and the administration of the incomes from the Duchy, were becoming more and more difficult. She was soon deeply in debt again and so she decided in 1663 to transfer the Duchy of Chevreuse and Dampierre to her son, the Duc de Luynes, in order, she declared, 'to free herself from the burden of supervising such large possessions', while he undertook to pay her debts and to allow her a suitable annuity. Moreover, she retained the right 'for herself and all her staff to stay in Dampierre at any time and to use all the furniture'. Then, three months later, the Duc de Luynes transferred the Duchy, also with the stipulation that he could continue to stay at Dampierre, to his son, the seventeen-year-old Charles-Honoré d'Albert, who now, with the permission of the King, became the new Duc de Chevreuse.

This grandson of Marie appeared to be unlike his father in that he was a man of action, eager to distinguish himself, and full of the promise of becoming a brave soldier. Marie's hopes for the glorious future of her family were now concentrated on him. As the grandson of the Constable of France, and now as Duc de Chevreuse, he was a member of the highest nobility in the country.

At that time the crown allied itself with the rich bourgeoisie instead of with the nobility. France was ruled by men of lowlier descent with a commercial background, and the King entrusted the highest positions in the Government to them, so that they should devote all their efforts to his interest alone. They did what was expected of them. However high he promoted them, they remained aware, not only of the fact that their exalted positions could be short-lived, but that in any case after their deaths their families would again return to their original lowly level, whilst the only possibility of preventing this was by marrying their children into noble families. Marie understood this prevailing trend and conceived the idea that her grandson should marry one of Colbert's daughters. It is possible that the rapid double-transfer of her Duchy, together with the title of Duc de Chevreuse, was already undertaken with this end in view.

Colbert was the son of a rich cloth-merchant, and although he had now become, as a chronicler wrote, 'a great man and in a limited way secretly ruled over the whole of Europe', he remained conscious of his origin, and a family connection with the highest nobility was for him a most desirable prospect. When the King honoured him with his agreement to the marriage of his daughter with the young Duc de Chevreuse, Colbert wrote to one of Marie's relatives: 'I give you the assurance that through this connection all my concern will be directed towards the interests of your house, for which I have always had the most sincere and warmest feelings.'

This marriage took place on February 1, 1667, with every display of splendour, and if it satisfied Colbert's ambitions, the advantages which it brought to the Luynes-Chevreuse family were still more evident and gave rise to a lot of comment at Court. Luynes could now expect a governorship and the young Duke could look forward to quick promotion in his military career, while Marie had complete security in the knowledge that the Duchy and Dampierre would be maintained in the best possible condition while she herself would spend the rest of her life in comfort and luxury together with her loyal friend and lover, de Laigue.

Although she no longer had anything to do with life at Court after Anne had died in January 1666, having spent four years of retirement in the convent of Val-de-Grâce, the Court did not forget Mme de Chevreuse. In the following year Bussy-Rabutin issued his satirical *Geographical Map of the Court*, and his reference to Marie gives a perfect picture of the atmosphere which now prevailed in the environment of the young Louis XIV and also of the attitude of the great nobles. He wrote:....

'Chevreuse is a large, already rather ancient fortress with completely decayed and neglected rooms; from the outside it is still quite imposing, but internally it is in a sad plight. Formerly it was very famous and often yielded to conquest, even by some foreign countries. But now, through the many sieges which it was forced to endure, the citadel is completely destroyed. It is said that it surrendered unconditionally many times. The occupants frequently changed and sometimes were very troublesome. Thus it has had many commanders, but now it is badly provided for, since the present owner is worth nothing at all!'

This last sneer was directed against the Marquis de Laigue whose health, although he was thirteen years younger than Marie, had long since been on the decline, so that he had many years previously made a will in which he left most of his possessions to her as well as a yearly income to the abbey of Port-Royal, where he wished to be buried. But they remained inseparable for another six years until his death, which left her completely alone.

She saw her son quite contented and happily married; she saw her grandson winning military honours in the wars of Louis XIV against Holland. Her ambitions for the future of her family were satisfied, but she herself was no longer needed by anyone. Instead of returning to a type of feudal state where traditional institutions tempered the power of the monarchy, which had been her aspiration, she now saw France as a strongly centralized country on the threshold of a period of glory. Under Colbert's protection of agriculture, industry and trade, French economy was developing and providing the means for the splendour of Louis XIV's reign. It appeared to be a united France, which had abolished regional differences and isolationism. Her ideas had been the product of an age that had passed. She had nothing more to do than to wait in peace and tranquillity for her death. And so Marie left Dampierre and retired to a convent, some miles from Paris, which had once been a Benedictine abbey. Here she spent five years in peace and solitude until she died at the age of seventy-nine. A provision in her will requested that her burial should take place without pomp, without funeral orations, without any ostentation, and that only a simple tombstone should be erected with only her name and the inscription:

'As humility has long since replaced in her heart a taste for the world's glamour and for the greatness of her time, she has forbidden that at her death any sign of that greatness should reappear, for she wishes to take it with her into the simplicity of this grave.'

However, the impression which her personality and activities had made upon her contemporaries was too strong for them to forget her; and as this was the period in which both participants in contemporary events and mere observers formed the habit of describing them in memoirs, notebooks and diaries, we everywhere find portraits of Mme de Chevreuse which, according to the attitude of the writer, vary widely, but always stress her importance, whether for good or ill.

One of the Mazarinades condemns her:

'All the world knows that she has initiated various grave disorders and that she was the heart and soul of a series of great designs; the trouble is only that one cannot ascribe a single good one to her. It is said that she could set everything in motion but never lead anything to a conclusion; she is perfectly capable of creating complications but never of resolving them. She knows full well how to extricate herself from a maze but only in order to get even deeper into another one. People are convinced that she manages to confuse everything hopelessly, and that is all that can be said of her.'

The Cardinal de Retz gives a very different picture of her in his memoirs, which he wrote in exile after his flight from imprisonment:

'I never saw another person in whom intuition could so take the place of judgement. She often suggested such brilliant expedients that they seemed like flashes of lightning, and were so wise that they would not be disowned by the greatest men of any age.'

But Saint-Simon's description of her personality goes perhaps deeper and is more comprehensive:

'Her charm and her beauty are great, but her recklessness is greater still, and all three are dominated by the power of her brain, which again is ruled by her insatiable ambition. She always has a clear judgement, sure and definite; she is always exciting, always imaginative and never lacking in hundreds of cunning stratagems; no ordeal can sap her energy and verve; her character has a male strength. In spite of her many affairs and adventures she remains constant in her heart. . . .'

Bibliography

Bailly, Auguste. *The Cardinal Dictator* (trans.), Cape, London 1936.
Batiffol, Louis. *La Duchesse de Chevreuse*, Paris, 1913.
——. *Le Cardinal de Retz*, Paris, 1927.
Belloc, Hilaire. *Richelieu*, Benn, London, 1930.
Boulenger, M. *Mazarin*, Paris, 1929.
Buchanan, Meriel. *Anne of Austria, the Infanta Queen*, Hutchinson, London, 1937.
Burckhardt, Carl: *Richelieu*, Munich, 1935.
Campbell, Dorothy de Brissac. *The Intriguing Duchess*, John Hamilton, 1931.
Capefigue, M. *Richelieu, Mazarin, la Fronde et le Régne de Louis XIV*, Paris, 1835.
Carré, Henri. *The Early life of Louis XIV* (trans.), Hutchinson, London, 1951.
Chéruel, P. A. *Histoire de France sous le ministère de Mazarin*, Paris, 1882.
Clark, Sir G. N. *The Seventeenth Century* 2nd edn, Clarendon Press, Oxford, 1947.
Cousin, Victor. *The Secret History of the French Court, or the Life and Times of Mme de Chevreuse* (trans.), Delisser & Procter, New York, 1859.
Federn, Karl. *Richelieu* (trans.), G. Allen & Unwin, London, 1928.
——. *Mazarin*, Munich, 1922.
Freer, Martha Walker. *The Regency of Anne of Austria*, London, 1866.
——. *The Married Life of Anne of Austria*, Eveleigh Nash, London, 1912.
Hazzall, Arthur. *Mazarin*. 1903.
Lodge, E. C. *Sully, Colbert and Turgot*, Methuen, London, 1931.
Lough, John. *An Introduction to Seventeenth Century France*, Longman, Green & Co., London, 1954.
Patmore, K. A. *The Court of Louis XIII*, Methuen, London, 1909.
Perkins, James B. *France under Richelieu and Mazarin*, 1913.
Robiquet, P. *Le Coeur d'une Reine*, Paris, 1912.
Tapié, V. L. *La France de Louis XIII et Richelieu*. 1952.
Taylor, I. A. *The Making of a King, Louis XIII*.
Todière, L. P. *La Fronde et Mazarin* 2nd edn, Tours, 1858.
Williams, Hugh Noel. *A Fair Conspirator*, Methuen, London, 1913.

Sources

Cabanes, Augustin. *The Secret Cabinet of History*. Edition 1897.

Mailly, J. B. *L'esprit de la Fronde*. 1772–73.

Fontenay-Mareuil. *Mémoires*. 1819.

Moreau, C. *Choix des Mazarinades*. 1853.

de Motteville, Langlois. *Memoirs for the History of Anne of Austria*. Edition 1726.

Cardinal de Retz. *Mémoires*. 1774.

Richelieu. *Mémoires*. 1810.

Richelieu. *Testament politique*. 1740.

La Rochefoucauld. *Mémoires de la Régence d'Anne d'Autriche*. 1688.

Tallement de Réaux. *Chronique Scandaleuse – Historiettes*. 1854.

Zeller, B. *Le Connétable de Luynes*. 1879.

Index